Grasping Globalization

Its Impact and Your Corporate Response

John L. Manzella

Published by

MANZELLA
TRADE COMMUNICATIONS, INC.

Published by

Manzella Trade Communications, Inc.

PO Box 1188, Williamsville, NY 14231-1188 U.S.A.

Tel: 716.681.8880 • Fax: 716.681.5678

www.ManzellaTrade.com • Info@ManzellaTrade.com

ISBN-13: 978-0-926566-06-4

ISBN-10: 0-926566-06-7

Library of Congress Control Number: 2005908485

For additional copies of this book, go to
www.GraspingGlobalization.com

Cover design by Jon Valerio

This book is dedicated to my wife, Karla, who not only edits my work but consistently supports my endeavors, and to my children, Lauren, Christopher, Victoria and Francesca, who I encourage to follow their dreams regardless of how difficult they may seem.

I would like to express my appreciation to all those who made this book possible. I am particularly grateful to the following individuals for their insightful comments, assistance and guidance: Jeff Belt, Bob Bissen, James Burroughs, Carl Chang, Larry Davidson, Christopher Falgiano, Daniel Griswold, Jeff Liebel, Jim Manzella, Tony Manzella, James McConnell, Al Moser, Paris F. Roselli, Gene Schreiber, John Slenker and Ralph Watkins.

Contents

Introduction

Globalization will impact you. And if you think you are isolated from this, think again.

The effects of today's global economic realities go far beyond the balance sheet. They are transforming our culture and political relationships, and in the process, impacting virtually every aspect of our lives. Consequently, no country, industry, business or individual is exempt. We all must adapt—and continue to adapt. For business, this means developing strategies that support worldwide expansion. But in the existing environment of fear and anxiety, how effectively executives communicate the impact of globalization on their company—and the logic behind their international business responses and decisions—can mean the difference between achieving understanding and support or experiencing suspicion and protest.

The Convergence of Powerful Forces Is Creating Fear and Insecurity

We are witnessing one of the greatest periods of transformation in history. The convergence of powerful technological, political, economic and cultural forces is shaping the 21st century. Nations, communities, companies and workers are finding it difficult to adapt—but truly necessary.

Technological advances in microelectronics, computers, telecommunications, transportation logistics, biotechnology and other fields are changing the way we live and work. The fall of Communism, which added one-third of humanity to the capitalistic ranks, is sharply boosting global competition and creating new markets. Globalization, made possible by the technological revolution, is empowering companies to source and sell anything anywhere. Concurrently, many traditional cultures are resisting the modernization pressures these changes bring. In response to these seemingly chaotic events, many faiths are retreating into religious fundamentalism in order to regain certainty in an uncertain world.

How did we get here?

Industrialization emerged in the late 1700s in Great Britain and early 1800s in the United States and Germany. The invention of the steam engine and its application to railroads enabled the speedy transport of mass produced goods across large distances. And the invention of electricity, which virtually turned night into day, established new paradigms. The recent integration of new technologies, global markets and improved supply chain management has again altered our production and distribution models with fantastic results. Productivity has climbed to new highs while innovation has flourished. The shift from brawn power—use of muscle on the factory floor—to brainpower is nearly complete. Today, self-directed workers operate in teams and apply more sophisticated skills to create and run new processes.

What is the result? Manufacturing output continues to rise while the number of workers, as well as inflation-adjusted prices, continue to fall. In turn, the manufacturing contribution to U.S. gross domestic product (GDP) is declining—from 22 percent in 1979 to 12.7 percent in 2004.

We've seen these trends before. In 1940, 9.5 million U.S. workers were employed on farms. By 2004, this number fell to approximately

2.2 million. Yet, U.S. agricultural output skyrocketed. In the process, the U.S. did not lose 7.3 million farm jobs: they shifted to emerging industries resulting in higher standards of living and a more prosperous economy. This fact has gone virtually unnoticed.

From 1970 through June 2005, the number of working Americans has grown by 63 million, a jump from 78.7 million to 141.6 million, according to the Bureau of Labor Statistics' Household data. And the Labor Department projects a net gain of 21.3 million jobs from 2002 through 2012. However, manufacturing jobs have fallen from a high of 21 million in 1979 to 14.3 million in June 2005. Many blame this on rising imports and offshoring. But analysis reveals that new technologies, high levels of productivity and improved manufacturing processes are the primary causes. Additionally, as more functions such as accounting, design and trucking, for example, are routinely contracted from manufacturing companies to local specialist accounting, design and trucking firms, the U.S. Census Bureau re-categorizes these jobs from manufacturing to services, lowering the overall manufacturing count, while raising the services count.

U.S. Employment, in Millions

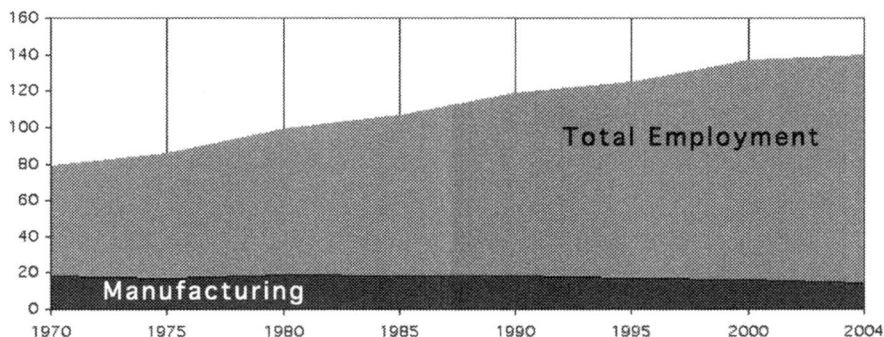

Source: U.S. Department of Labor

Job losses, as reported in the daily newspaper, often give the impression of mounting losses. But consider this. Normal U.S. job churn results in the average loss of 31 million jobs annually. What's not reported is even more important: new jobs are created even faster—but not of the heavy manufacturing vintage. In turn, resources are shifting from low-technology production to higher value, higher technology processes that create new industries and higher skilled, higher paying jobs. This pattern is not new—and not well understood.

Looking forward, U.S. manufacturers must compete less on price and more on product design, branding strategies, productivity, flexibility, quality and responsiveness to customer needs. This puts a high premium on skills. Consequently, it's no surprise that unemployment is higher among workers with lower levels of education. For example, in April 2005, the U.S. unemployment rate for workers age 25 years and older without a high school diploma was 8.4 percent. It declined to 4.4 percent for high school graduates, 3.9 percent for those with some college education or an Associates degree, and 2.5 percent for college graduates or higher.

In an attempt to adapt to globalization, companies are increasingly specializing in more complex, value-added goods and services. In turn, workers are seeking greater expertise. This pattern, however, is not without consequences. The previous shift from an agrarian society to an industrial economy compelled workers to leave farms in search of factory jobs. Workers were required to learn new skills. But the skills demanded today are far more sophisticated, and probably are creating even more fear and anxiety than before. This is causing a backlash.

As the U.S. manufacturing sector evolves, less competitive industries will increasingly demand protection via creative subsidies, quotas and regulations from policymakers. Higher tariffs will be more difficult to obtain. In the past, different tactics were used in an attempt to isolate industries from competition. For example, in the early 19th century, the English Luddites destroyed textile machines because they replaced weavers.

Federal Reserve Chairman Alan Greenspan has repeatedly warned that creeping protectionism must be thwarted and reversed. In testimony before the U.S. Senate Committee on Finance on June 23, 2005, Chairman Greenspan said, "Any significant elevation of tariffs that substantially reduces our overall imports, by keeping out competitively priced goods, would materially lower our standard of living. A return to protectionism would threaten the continuation of much of the extraordinary growth in living standards worldwide, but especially in the United States, that is due importantly to the post-World War II opening of global markets. Such an initiative would send the adverse message to our trading partners that the United States, while accepting the benefits of broadened world trade, is not willing to absorb the structural adjustments that are often necessary." Through pro-globalist advocacy efforts, corporate America must take it upon itself to fight protectionism and educate various audiences on today's economic realities.

For example, trade and globalization have generated an increase in U.S. income of approximately $1 trillion annually, measured in 2003 dollars. This translates into an income gain of about $10,000 for the average American household per year, according to Gary Clyde Hufbauer of the Institute for International Economics, a Washington, D.C., think tank. And further liberalization that achieves global free trade and investment could produce another $500 billion in U.S. income annually or $5,000 per household each year, Hufbauer says.

The bottom line: to remain competitive, companies must become more specialized and expand internationally. This may involve establishing a joint venture or strategic alliance in a foreign market, acquiring an overseas firm through direct investment or licensing technology abroad. But in this environment of suspicion and fear, poorly communicating a decision to move facilities abroad, for example, will result in negative publicity and community ill will. Protests, loss of support from politicians and consumer boycotts may even ensue. This can be avoided.

This book will provide you with an understanding of the real impact of globalization, and explain how you can more persuasively communicate your corporate responses and sensitive decisions to the media, policymakers, employees and investors.

Part I

Understanding Today's Global Realities

Globalization is a dynamic process that involves the integration of national markets through international trade, foreign direct investment and portfolio investment. Based on free-market capitalism and powered by advances in telecommunications, transportation and finance, globalization enables companies and individuals to establish relationships anywhere in the world. In addition, it provides billions of people worldwide the means to obtain a higher standard of living.

In their book *A Future Perfect*, John Micklethwait and Adrian Wooldridge argue that globalization increases people's freedom to shape their identities and sharpen their talents. It allows consumers to buy the best the world has to offer, while giving producers the tools to find buyers and partners worldwide. As a result, companies and individuals are empowered to generate new wealth in ways undreamed of just a few years ago. But it's also creating much controversy.

Other trends already have changed the nature of competitive advantage. And in this period of great transformation from a familiar system to an unfamiliar one, new paradigms are emerging as old ones fade. For example, for centuries an abundance of natural resources was known to secure a nation's competitive advantage. This is no longer the case. Japan, Hong Kong and other countries and regions of wealth with few natural resources clearly have disproved this. Today, knowledge and information have become the new generator of competitive advantage. This is becoming more evident in every industry.

Many of our largest corporations, that for decades dominated the economic landscape, are being pushed aside by leaner, more knowledge-intensive companies. And since knowledge and skill are infinite resources, obtainable by both large and small companies alike, smaller companies are not disadvantaged by their size. As a result, a real sustainable competitive advantage is the ability of a small company's workforce to learn faster than the competition.

Change, which is often accompanied by fear and disorganization, is not easy. But with change come new challenges and exciting opportunities. For companies and their employees to succeed well into the future, it is necessary for them to grasp the new economic realities that globalization brings, and embrace—not reject—the challenges they present.

The Perception of Outsourcing Is Inaccurate

Several decades ago, as Albert Einstein monitored an exam for a graduate level physics class, a student raised his hand and said there was a problem: the questions on the exam were the same as the previous year's test. Einstein agreed. The questions were indeed the same, but in a year's time the answers had changed completely. Given the accelerated pace of change today, the "answers" are not just different from those of last year. In many cases, they are even different from those of last month.

Many Americans, as well as Members of Congress on both sides of the aisle, do not understand why some answers that seemed appropriate only a few years ago do not apply today. On the other hand, some do indeed understand, but choose not to accept the new realities. For example, several policymakers have revealed to this author that taking a globalist view in support of international trade is dangerous to their job security. In fact, one Member of Congress said he understood the need for some companies to outsource services abroad, but could not sell that reality back home. When it comes to outsourcing abroad, also known as offshoring, many politicians are basing their policy decisions on outdated assumptions that may sell in their Congressional districts. But in the end, these anti-globalist positions actually will hurt, not help their constituents.

The fear that offshoring will result in fewer good jobs for American workers is understandable since some activities include the movement of knowledge-intensive services to India and other countries with educated, less expensive, English-speaking labor pools. But careful analysis reveals that worldwide sourcing—made possible by new technologies that digitize and cheaply transmit information around the world—provides real benefits. Unfortunately, little evidence of this has been publicized. And when companies communicate a strategy to outsource certain services via a public relations campaign, they often do so poorly. This does not help. In turn, due to misinformation about offshoring, fear of negative publicity, political pressure, investor objections or employee criticism, many companies have either cancelled or not executed offshoring contracts. Many state agencies have incurred the same problems and turned a blind eye to offshoring opportunities that could have saved their tax payers millions of dollars—funds desperately needed!

If placed in the larger context, offshoring is seen as one of several means by which jobs are lost in the short-term. History tells us that new technologies and improved business strategies displace jobs. For example, automobile workers replaced buggy makers, while ATMs, voice mail and voice recognition software eliminated bank teller, receptionist and medical transcription jobs. As pointed out earlier, the U.S. economy loses an average of 31 million jobs annually. But new jobs are created more quickly than old ones are lost. New technologies, innovation and higher productivity, the primary causes of job turnover, also known as job churn, actually increase wages and improve living standards. In turn, new industries and higher skilled jobs emerge. Thus, Forrester Research's estimate of 3.3 million service jobs moving offshore by 2015 represents a small fraction of job churn. How many Americans are familiar with this reality?

Lower-tech jobs most likely to be outsourced, such as bookkeeping and customer service, are projected to increase in the United States. And higher-tech jobs prone to outsourcing, like computer programming and software design, also are expected to increase here, according to the Labor Department. In fact, from 2002 through 2012, all U.S. computer-related occupations are estimated to grow by 15 to 57 percent. That's not all. Many back office jobs (some more skilled than others) are estimated to grow in the United States. For example, paralegal jobs are projected to increase by 28.7 percent, bill and account collector positions are estimated to grow by 24.5 percent, customer service representative occupations are estimated to increase by 24.3 percent, radiologist jobs (which are part of the larger medical field) are anticipated to rise by 19.5 percent, accountant and auditor positions are projected to expand by 19.5 percent, architectural occupations are projected to expand by 17.3 percent and commercial and industrial designer jobs are projected to grow by 14.7 percent.

How does offshoring lead to better jobs? The McKinsey Global Institute estimates two-thirds of economic benefits from outsourcing services to India flow back here. Firms that outsource generate higher profits, have more capital to invest in R&D, become more globally competitive and are better positioned to expand sales worldwide— creating higher-paid jobs.

In March 2004, The Information Technology Association of America (ITAA), a leading U.S. trade association for the IT industry, released *The Impact of Offshore IT Software and Services Outsourcing on the U.S. Economy and the IT Industry*. According to ITAA, the study conclusively demonstrates that worldwide sourcing of computer software and services increases the number of U.S. jobs, improves real wages for American workers, and pushes the U.S. economy to perform at a higher level, thereby generating many other economic benefits.

Global Insight, a leading economic analysis, forecasting and financial information company, was commissioned by ITAA to conduct the study. The Global Insight research team was led by Global Insight Chief Economist Dr. Nariman Behravesh, one of the world's most accurate economic forecasters. Nobel Prize winning economist Dr. Lawrence R. Klein, the founder of Wharton Econometric Forecasting Associates (WEFA), Inc. and a Global Insight associate, also made significant contributions to the study.

"We have long held the position that global sourcing creates more jobs and higher real wages for American workers," said ITAA President Harris N. Miller. "Now we have the data that prove it. Far from being an economic tsunami that washes away domestic IT employment as some believe, global sourcing helps companies become more productive and competitive. The savings produced through worldwide sourcing are invested in new products and services, in new market expansion, and, most importantly, in creating new jobs and increasing real wages for American workers. This research replaces fear with sound economic analysis, allowing for an informed approach to the global marketplace."

The ITAA/Global Insight study found:
- Worldwide sourcing of IT services and software generated an additional 90,000 U.S. jobs in 2003; by 2008, net new jobs are estimated to total 317,000.
- Global sourcing adds to the take-home pay of average U.S. workers. With inflation kept low and productivity high,

worldwide sourcing is projected to increase real wages in the U.S. by 0.44 percent in 2008.

- Worldwide sourcing contributes significantly to real U.S. GDP, adding $33.6 billion in 2003. By 2008, real GDP is predicted to be $124.2 billion higher than it would be in an environment in which offshore IT software and services outsourcing did not occur.
- Global sourcing contributed $2.3 billion to U.S. exports in 2003 and is projected to contribute $9 billion by 2008.

The study also found that raising barriers to worldwide sourcing would adversely impact U.S. workers and U.S. firms. If all global sourcing of software and IT services terminated completely, the report said, the impact would slow the U.S. economy and reduce the number of new jobs available to American workers. While worldwide sourcing is expected to increase jobs and wages, Miller said much needs to be done to address the challenges of those workers displaced by this economic shift. The report offers a range of recommendations to achieve this.

Catherine Mann of the Institute for International Economics says offshoring of computer manufacturing resulted in a 10 to 30 percent drop in computer costs. In turn, sales of PCs soared. This led to a rapid rise in U.S. productivity and added $230 billion in cumulative GDP from 1995 through 2002. The result: many new jobs emerged, far exceeding those lost to outsourcing.

If applied to select medical services and other fields, offshoring could reduce costs and generate new waves of innovation, resulting in better jobs not yet imagined. As Ross Perot's early 1990s forecast of a "giant sucking sound" proved incorrect, so is the fear of offshoring. In reality, the U.S. service sector will significantly expand. And since the industry has become more sophisticated, average hourly earnings for service production workers have already caught up to those in manufacturing. Nevertheless, service jobs that require left-brained routine quantitative functions, not intuitive or creative problem solving skills, will increasingly be automated or moved offshore. As a result, those jobs that are lost will increasingly be featured on prime-time news and create the false impression that the American service industry, as a whole, is moving to India.

In the end, these false impressions can be powerful. According to the National Foundation for American Policy, a Washington, D.C. research organization, as of March 17, 2005, there were 112 bills in 40 states designed to restrict outsourcing. On the same date in 2004, there were 107 bills in 33 states. If successful, in the long run, these bills will harm the workers they are intended to help. Stated in the 2005 McKinsey Global Institute report, *How Offshoring of Services Could Benefit France*, "A new dynamic is emerging in the economic sectors exposed to global competition: early movers in offshoring improve their cost position and boost their market share, creating new jobs in the process. Companies who resist the trend will see increasingly unfavorable cost positions that erode market share and eventually end in job destruction. This is why adopting protectionist policies to stop companies from offshoring would be a mistake. Offshoring is a powerful way for companies to reduce their costs and improve the quality and kinds of products they offer consumers, allowing them to invest in the next generation of technology and create the jobs of tomorrow."

As business becomes more competitive, companies increasingly will focus on their core strengths and contract out functions that can be provided more efficiently by others. Many of these functions will be offshored. But more will be outsourced within the United States. This provides many opportunities for regions with various advantages. Take Western New York for example. The State University of New York at Buffalo, as well as many other local universities and colleges, graduate tremendous numbers of very well educated students each year. In the Western New York area, housing and corporate real estate costs are among the lowest in the country. The region also has one of the largest international trade and transportation infrastructures, and the quality of life is top notch. According to Jeff Belt, president of Acen, a Buffalo, N.Y.-based software development and web hosting company, "The cost to operate a software firm in Western New York is 48 percent less than in metropolitan Seattle, and all the necessary talent and infrastructure are here."

Based on these realities, Western New York is naturally suited to attract culturally-sensitive, high-skilled back office operations that require elevated levels of quality control. The target: corporations that operate skilled back office service operations (knowledge-intensive jobs not requiring face-to-face contact) currently located in high-cost metropolitan areas such as New York City, Boston and Washington, D.C. Based on Western New York's advantages that most regions cannot match, it has an opportunity to brand itself as "America's insourcing center" and position itself as the high-end "American Bangalore," free of cultural disconnects, long-distance management problems and political uncertainties caused by Indian-Pakistan tensions and global terrorism. Plus, Western New York offers Manhattan-based financial firms a well-suited data back-up location that exceeds the 200-300 mile distance recommended by the federal government's interagency white paper on strengthening the resilience of the U.S. financial system. Like so many other U.S. regions, however, Western New York needs to better adapt to new global economic realities in order to seize valuable opportunities within its reach.

The Chinese Challenge Is Creating Fear

China's accession to the World Trade Organization (WTO) in December 2001 has advanced U.S. interests in many ways. For example, China certainly has had human rights problems. However, China's free market reforms over the last two decades unquestionably have contributed to greater economic and political freedom for the Chinese people. Far from rewarding China for bad behavior, WTO accession has accelerated those reforms, and correspondingly, accelerated the liberalization of Chinese society.

Through expanded trade, WTO accession also has empowered China's fast-growing entrepreneurial class to put greater pressure on Chinese authority from the inside out. This strategy is not unique. Once markets are liberalized, their political systems follow. The adage "open markets open minds" is true. To validate this, all one has to do is look at Mexico. Prior to the North American Free Trade Agreement (NAFTA), that country's ruling party, the PRI, had a decades-long indisputable grip on the country. Since NAFTA implementation, the PRI power structure has dwindled considerably as demonstrated by the election of Mexican President Vicente Fox, a member of the National Action Party.

For a quarter-century, U.S. trade has helped change China by supporting economic freedom, human rights, access to information, higher living standards and the rule of law for the Chinese people. And, with today's technology, this change will continue to accelerate. Through a policy of engagement the United States has infused ideas and values into Chinese society. On the other hand, to determine how well non-engagement or isolationist policies work, look no further than North Korea and Cuba: two countries where the United States has virtually no trade—and no influence.

Since the fear of "Red China" has subsided, an economic-based fear has emerged. Prior to acceding to the WTO, China already had access to U.S. markets. In fact, supporting China's membership in the WTO did not change U.S. tariff rates on Chinese goods. Instead, WTO membership forced China to open its marketplace. Under the accession agreement, China agreed to cut average tariffs from 24 percent to 9 percent by 2005, further cut tariffs on U.S. priority goods to 7 percent by 2003, eliminate tariffs on high-technology goods by 2005, cut average agricultural tariffs by half, and remove China's distribution monopoly, allowing U.S. firms to freely distribute their goods in China. With China's population of more than 1.3 billion, the United States could not afford to be locked out of this emerging market.

Within a few years of China joining the WTO, the effects of Chinese tariff reductions on U.S. and third country goods already were evident. China's increasingly strong demand for oil, industrial metals and other commodities, as well as semi-finished goods, boosted its import growth considerably. As a result, China has become the United States' fifth largest export destination. If Hong Kong were added, China would be in fourth place. And from 1999 to 2004, U.S. exports to China increased nearly 10 times faster than U.S. exports to the rest of the world.

But China's growing impact on the trade scene is not just affecting the United States. In 2004, China became the world's third largest importer and exporter of merchandise trade, according to the WTO. In fact, its world imports reached $561 billion in 2004, $106 billion more than Japan's. Its world exports rose to $593 billion, $28 billion more than Japan's. But the large U.S. trade deficit with China, combined with the movement of U.S. manufacturing jobs there, has America scared.

In 2004, the U.S.-China trade deficit reached $162 billion, the largest among U.S. trade partners. This partly reflects a shift in U.S. imports of labor-intensive products away from higher-wage Asian countries to lower-wage China. The result: U.S. imports from China

Total U.S.-China Trade in Goods, in Billions

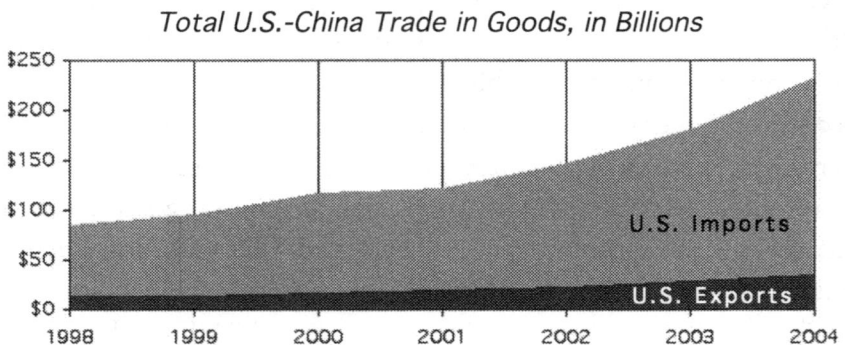

Source: U.S. Department of Commerce

have risen while U.S. imports from the rest of Asia have flattened. Nevertheless, the U.S. deficit with China continues to be a major concern.

Global FDI, which continues to pour into China, also is raising eyebrows. In fact, in 2003, China attracted more FDI than the United States, according to The PRS Group, Inc., a publisher of political, economic, and financial risk ratings for 140 countries, based in East Syracuse, New York. And due to China's new WTO-mandated reforms and trade liberalization measures, more FDI is anticipated to flow into China's manufacturing industry, the sector which already receives the majority of capital. This may be at the expense of Asian developing countries, and perhaps Mexico and Central America. Another concern is that an increasing share of this investment is flowing into higher value-added sectors such as semiconductors.

A growing number of foreign component suppliers also are establishing facilities in China—a precursor to the emergence of an FDI-led integrated supply base. A strong domestic supply chain, something Mexico, for example, has not been able to establish, is another important factor helping to position China as an increasingly attractive destination for manufacturing FDI. Additional factors, including lower costs for labor, energy, water and taxes, as

Global Foreign Direct Investment in China, in Billions

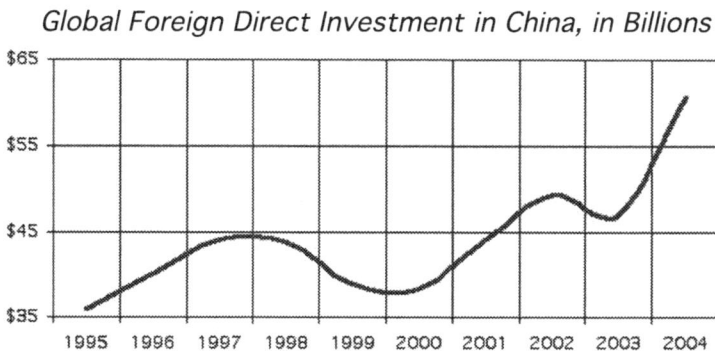

Source: The PRS Group, Inc.

well as subsidized inputs, have led to a shifting of sourcing from Mexico to China for apparel, electronic products and telephone equipment, according to Ralph Watkins, U.S. International Trade Commission's Program Manager for Production Sharing. As the demand for these products increases, more investment in Chinese plants and equipment is almost certain.

With the opening of China's markets, U.S., European and other companies plan to export more goods to China in coming years. As this occurs, even more FDI is expected to flow into China for the purpose of establishing sales and service facilities. In turn, these companies likely will source more of their goods from within China.

Is China satisfying its WTO commitments? The opinions are mixed. China's implementation efforts have been impressive, but its compliance has been uneven and incomplete. A sensitive issue that has received a great deal of attention is the Chinese piracy of U.S. intellectual property. In turn, the Bush administration has indicated that intellectual property protection is a top priority, among many others, and has called on the Chinese government to take specific measures to improve a situation that many believe is costing U.S. companies tens of billions of dollars each year. On July 22, 2005, the Bush administration also created a senior position to help combat intellectual property violations. The Office of the Coordinator for International Intellectual Property Enforcement will be located at the Department of Commerce.

Another very sensitive issue involves China's practice of not allowing its currency (the yuan, also known as the renminbi), to float freely. For more than a decade, China pegged the yuan to the U.S. dollar. This provided financial stability, helping China to weather the Asian financial crisis in 1997 and 1998. However, on July 21, 2005 the Chinese government announced a change in its exchange rate regime from the fixed peg close to 8.28 per U.S. dollar to a managed float based on a basket of currencies. Upon this news, Donald Johnston, Secretary-General of the Organisation for Economic

Co-operation and Development (OECD), a forum composed of 30 market democracies, said the measure is "in line with China's determined efforts to build a market-based economy." Although this represents only a modest adjustment, China is moving in the right direction. But the question begs, is it enough for now?

For quite some time, U.S. Congressional sources have declared the yuan to be considerably undervalued, which in turn, makes Chinese exports more attractive worldwide. In response, some U.S. politicians and various organizations have suggested that China should allow the yuan to float freely, assuming it will rise to a higher level. On the other hand, some economists believe that if this were to occur, the currency may become volatile due to China's fragile financial sector, instability associated with the country's transition to a market economy and difficult economic adjustments associated with WTO-mandated reforms. In turn, a widely fluctuating yuan could have a destabilizing effect and fall well below current levels, leading to a financial crisis.

Nevertheless, a revaluation of the yuan is likely to have little impact on the U.S. trade deficit. Why? If the yuan were to rise in value, U.S. companies would continue to seek low cost imports from other developing countries. In his June 23, 2005 testimony before the U.S. Senate Committee on Finance, Chairman Greenspan said, "An increase in the exchange rate of the renminbi, relative to the dollar, would likely redirect trade within Asia, reversing to some extent the patterns that have emerged during the past half century. However, a revaluation of the renminbi would have limited consequences for overall U.S. imports, as well as for U.S. exports that compete with Chinese products for third markets." On the other hand, according to the Deloitte Research report, *China at a Crossroads: Seven Risks of Doing Business*, a revaluation would allow other Asian countries to become more comfortable in allowing their currencies to appreciate against the dollar, a move that would ultimately result in an improvement of the U.S. current account balance. How much? Economists suggest it would be minimal. (Interestingly, on July 21, 2005, Malaysia also announced a change to its foreign exchange regime to a managed basket float).

Although the full impact of a floating yuan is uncertain, many analysts agree that pegging the yuan to the dollar also has had negative consequences for China. In a May 2005 report to Congress, prior to China's announcement of the new managed float based on a basket of currencies, the U.S. Treasury Department said the yuan's peg "blocks the transmission of critical price signals, impedes needed adjustment of international imbalances, attracts speculative capital flows and is a large and increasing risk to the Chinese economy." It also is widely agreed that the pegging policy has hurt low-cost global producers who compete with China for global marketshare.

The yuan-dollar pegging policy originally began when the dollar was strong and China was considered an economy in need of development aid. Now that China has become a stronger international player, especially in the manufacturing sector, and one that is seeking higher technologies, China's new currency policy is welcome—with the hope that China allows for greater currency flexibility in the near future.

The most important issue, which perhaps is at the core of all concerns, revolves around China's growing economic might. From 1980 through 1990, China's GDP growth averaged 10.1 percent annually. From 1990 through 1999, it increased to 10.7 percent, among the highest in the world. And Chinese growth continues to be exceptional. As of 2004, China's GDP was 14 percent of that of the United States and 4 percent of the world's. But this is changing quickly. A Goldman Sachs report predicts China's economy could exceed the United States' by 2039.

Already the world leading supplier of labor-intensive sewn products, in 2003 China supplied 75 percent of U.S. imports of toys, dolls, games, sporting goods and bicycles; 68 percent of footwear and luggage; 63 percent of lamps; 42 percent of furniture; 41 percent of consumer electronics other than TVs; 35 percent of household appliances; and 29 percent of computer hardware, according to Watkins.

The World's Factory: China Enters the 21st Century, a 2004 Deloitte Research report, indicated that China produced more than 50 percent of the world's cameras, 30 percent of air conditioners and televisions, 25 percent of washing machines, and almost 20 percent of refrigerators.

Importantly, the January 1, 2005 elimination of world quotas on textiles and apparel will result in a greater shift of apparel and textile production away from numerous existing world suppliers to China. Why? The WTO estimates that the U.S. quota on Chinese imports of apparel had the equivalent effect of a 34 percent tax on Chinese imports, much higher than other suppliers, according to the Deloitte Research report *China at Crossroads: Seven Risks of Doing Business.* By eliminating this tax (assuming no change in barriers or currency valuation occurs), China's share of U.S. apparel imports is anticipated to jump from 16 percent to 50 percent. In turn, China's share of the U.S. apparel market is projected to rise from 5.4 percent to 22.5 percent. The report further notes that India's share of this import market also is expected to rise dramatically, from 4 percent to 15 percent. Consequently, many other countries are predicted to

China's Real GDP Growth Rate, in Percentages

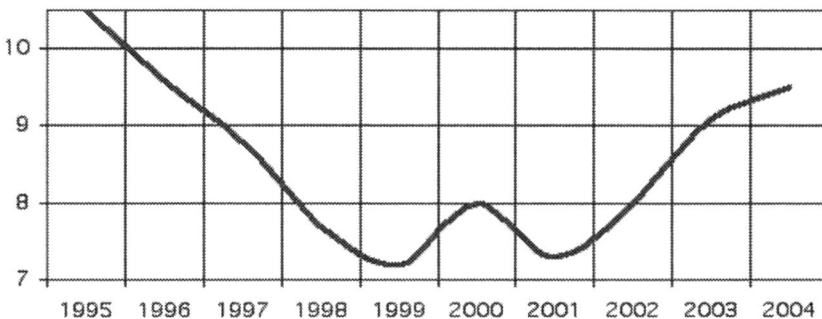

Source: The PRS Group, Inc.

experience a large drop in share of apparel exports to the United States, including Mexico, Bangladesh and the Philippines.

A 2005 Deloitte Research survey of 226 U.S.-based manufacturing multinationals with combined revenues of $500 billion revealed that over the next two years 55.7 percent of respondents plan to enter or expand marketing/sales operations in China, 57.1 percent plan to source goods there, 38.4 percent plan to conduct some manufacturing there, and 25.6 percent plan to conduct some engineering/R&D activity in China. It is expected that China will continue to move up the value chain, with higher technology products becoming an increasing share of its output and exports. How high up is unknown. However, investors indicate they continue to resist transferring their highest value-added operations to China.

Growing the Global Corporation: Global Investment Trends of U.S. Manufacturers, another Deloitte report, indicates that U.S. manufacturing FDI in developing countries, including China, was 32 percent in 1999, 25 percent in 2000, 22 percent in 2001, 7 percent in 2002 and 15 percent in 2003. Although currently relatively small, over time U.S. manufacturing FDI in China is expected to rise. As this occurs, China will become the world's manufacturer for a large variety of goods. In the short-term, the primary objective of Chinese producers will be to make goods less expensively for global markets; in the longer-term, the main objective will be to supply the domestic market. Thus, as Chinese internal development continues to push westward across the country, domestic demand will skyrocket transforming China into one of the world's biggest markets. Consequently, some analysts predict that much of Chinese production currently being exported will be consumed domestically. In turn, smaller developing countries will be delighted to pick up the export slack and satisfy global demand.

Although China's political challenges are massive, its 1.3 billion consumers will continue to provide U.S. exporters and investors with tremendous opportunities. In terms of production sharing (the allocation of different stages of the manufacturing process to different countries), Chinese companies will increasingly team with U.S. manufacturers to produce more globally attractive products. Although this strategy is likely to continue to lead to lower-tech manufacturing jobs losses, it is anticipated to grow more jobs in capital-intensive manufacturing, product development, design, and marketing-related activities in the U.S. And according to the U.S. International Trade Commission, production sharing is responsible for generating new jobs and retaining those that would be lost due to intense foreign competition.

Overall, China is presenting new opportunities, as well as new risks. To remain competitive with China and the rest of the world, the American educational system must increasingly graduate skilled students who can compete in this new environment. According to the report, *Keeping America Competitive: How a Talent Shortage Threatens U.S. Manufacturing*, published by the National Association of Manufacturers, intense competition from the globalization of the manu- facturing marketplace, changing demographics and the relentless advancement of technology have challenged U.S manufacturing. "The result has been a dramatic increase in the sector's need for highly skilled, technically savvy employees who can fully exploit the productive potential of advanced technologies and support increased quality and product complexity. This need, in turn, has generated a talent shortage—from engineers and R&D professionals to skilled production workers and plant managers."

Shifting Demographics Are Influencing
Where Tomorrow's Facilities Will Be Built

Global demographics are shifting at an accelerated pace. This is causing certain national markets to expand while others contract— all while shaping the world economy. Increasing consumer income in a national market quickly translates into greater demand for goods and services there. In turn, that country is likely to attract more foreign direct investment.

In other countries, a rising median age affects consumer needs, preferences and tastes, and also impacts demand. As this occurs, companies continuously monitor where their markets—or moving targets—are growing and shrinking. In response, many move production and service facilities closer to the expanding markets in order to better serve them. These realities are not always easy to explain in an environment that is suspect of corporate motives.

According to the U.S. Census Bureau, the world's total population surpassed 6.4 billion in January 2005 and is anticipated to exceed 7 billion by 2013. Where these people live will influence decisions by American companies as to where to build their future production facilities. For example, companies sometimes choose to produce goods and services in the foreign country in order to eliminate ocean transportation costs, tariff barriers and other costs. Plus, proximity often enables companies to gather better intelligence on changing market conditions so they can quickly adjust. This is why foreign-owned multinationals operate in the United States. And according to *Insourcing Jobs: Making the Global Economy Work for America*, by Professor Matthew J. Slaughter of the Dartmouth College Tuck School of Business, these foreign companies employed 5.4 million Americans with a U.S. payroll of $307 billion in 2002.

Following long-established geographic and cultural patterns, almost all the net population growth—the difference between births and deaths—will occur in developing countries located in Asia, Latin America and Africa. For example, by 2013, China's population is expected to reach almost 1.4 billion, followed by India's, projected at 1.2 billion. Indonesia follows at 268 million, Brazil at 201 million, Pakistan at 190 million, and Bangladesh at 169 million.

Average per capita income in developing countries is understandably low as compared to developed countries. In 2005, for example, GDP per capita or income is estimated at approximately

$41,700 for each American, according to the International Monetary Fund. On the other hand, per capita income is approximately $6,500 in Mexico, $1,340 in China and only $620 in India. Based on these figures, anti-trade organizations often conclude that consumers in these countries cannot afford American products or services. Should U.S. companies subscribe to this logic, they will be at a loss. In terms of buying power, general per capita income figures can be misleading. For instance, India is estimated to have a middle class of more than 200 million people with the same purchasing power as the U.S. middle class. And according to Robert Wu, a consultant who works with Chinese and American firms, "China has 200 to 300 million people living in urban areas with considerable consumption capacity." For just about all U.S. exporters and investors, a new and relatively affluent market of 200 to 300 million plus consumers is well worth pursuing.

Additionally, the average life span continues to rise, and is projected to increase from 64 years in 2002 to 69 years by 2025, and to 77 years by 2050, according to the U.S. Census Bureau. This increased longevity has contributed to global population growth and is leading to a shifting age demographic characterized by higher proportions of the elderly. As a result, over the next two decades the age structure of world population will continue to shift, with older age groups making up an increasingly larger share of the total. In fact, the number of people age 65 and over is estimated to more than double. The greatest relative increase will occur in developing countries, while the largest absolute change will take place in Asia. The bottom line: by 2020, two-thirds of the world's elderly will live in developing countries.

As this age shift occurs, the elderly population in the United States and the rest of the developed world will increase by more than 50 percent. Concurrently, demand for products and services designed to satisfy the needs of this group will increase. For example, Americans over the age of 50 tend to use significantly more pharmaceutical products than any other segment of the population. As the world's population continues to age in both developed and developing countries, the demand for health-related products, as well as home care, is anticipated to skyrocket. In response, many U.S. companies that produce health related products and services are likely to relocate facilities in proximity to this expanding market.

As the elderly population grows in numbers, the median age of the world's people will continue to rise as well. Not to be confused with average age, the median means half of the population will be above and half below the age cited. In 1998, the median age was 24 in less developed nations, and 37 in more developed countries. However, by 2025, the median ages will rise to 30 and 43, respectively. Keep in mind: these people will grow up in an increasingly sophisticated age in terms of technology, communications and consumer products. Many of these age groups will be influenced by American culture; as youngsters they will listen to American music, watch American movies and wear American blue jeans. This also is a generation that will be better educated and enjoy a more affluent lifestyle.

What implications does this have for consumer spending? According to Harry S. Dent, Jr., author of *The Roaring 2000s Investor*, on average, Americans enter the workforce at age 19, get married at age 25.5 (27 for men and 24 for women), bear their first children two years later, and purchase their first homes at age 33 or 34. They trade up to the largest homes they'll own by 44, and fully furnish them by age 46.5 or 47. Interestingly, the average American also reaches peak spending at about 46, the same time the kids leave home. Dent observes that empty-nest couples then spend more on vacation homes, travel and leisure. They also become prospects for investment services and products as they approach retirement age.

Spending patterns in other developed nations are similar to those in the United States. As a result, it's reasonable to assume that as the median age rises and life expectancy increases in developed countries, from 76 years in 2002 to 80 years by 2025 according to the U.S. Census Bureau, consumer spending also will rise. Depending on a company's products or services, relocating facilities within close reach of these growing markets may be recognized as a sound strategic decision in the business community, but may be labeled as anti-American in the political community.

By studying shifts in world demographics, a company can pinpoint where tomorrow's major populations will live, identify the fastest-growing age groups (an important indicator of tastes and needs) and predict, based on similar demographics elsewhere, demand for certain products or services. In turn, this will influence where a company's next factories or service centers will be built.

European Union Expansion Will
Impact U.S. Investment Decisions

After World War II and throughout the Cold War period, the United States was unquestionably the world leader in terms of political and economic policy. In fact, the Cold War provided much of the glue that held the American-Western European alliance together. Since the end of the Cold War, and in light of European Union (EU) expansion, as well as contentious trade disputes, it appears that the United States is no longer in a position of dominance. This will affect the United States' ability to forge new political and economic policies that involve Europe and the rest of the world. This also will affect U.S. investment decisions.

On May 1, 2004, the EU welcomed 10 new countries, bringing the total number of members to 25 and increasing its total number of consumers from 375 million to 448 million. The world's largest single economy now has a combined output of $13 trillion annually, according to the Progressive Policy Institute, a Washington, D.C., pro-trade think tank associated with the New Democrats.

As part of their accession agreement, the new EU members—the Czech Republic, Hungary, Poland, the Slovak Republic, Slovenia, the Baltic states of Estonia, Latvia and Lithuania, and the Mediterranean islands of Malta and Cyprus—will continue to adopt the EU's common commercial policy and higher regulatory standards. In addition, they will adhere to EU bilateral trade agreements and apply its common external tariff. And, since most new members are located in Central Europe, their accession has erased the last traces of the old "Iron Curtain" from the Cold War years.

The original EU members also will have new responsibilities, many which may prove difficult. For example, since living standards and productivity levels of most new members are well below those of the original 15, billions of dollars in subsidies will be required to be transferred from the West to the East. And not unlike some of the problems that plagued former West Germany when it absorbed former East Germany, tensions will rise when workers in the West lose jobs to those in the accession countries. On the other hand, tensions also will rise in the East when jobs are lost to more productive workers in the West.

As new members apply the common EU external tariff, most U.S. products exported to these countries will be assessed a lower, not higher duty. In addition, since one set of standards and regulations now will apply to all 25 EU members, U.S. exporters selling to the new members will no longer have to navigate through 10 complex and often confusing regulatory environments. However, there is a downside.

Since products traded among the original 15 and 10 new EU participants are no longer assessed tariffs, intra-EU trade is likely to increase. Consequently, U.S. products exported to Central Europe, which are still subject to EU tariffs, albeit lower, are likely to become less competitive. The result: Europeans may buy more goods from each other and fewer from the U.S. and third countries—a phenomena known as trade diversion. As a result, this is likely to spur increased

U.S. investment in the EU and will translate into more U.S. companies establishing facilities there.

Although the rejection of the EU constitution by the French on May 29 and Dutch on June 1, 2005 may have slowed further European integration efforts, the EU, as well as an emerging Asian bloc led by China, will continue to expand and gain influence over the long term. These developments will continue to have a profound impact on where American companies direct their overseas investments and build their manufacturing facilities and service centers.

The Backlash

Since the emergence of local, regional and national economies, there has been a constant evolution in the stages of cultural and economic development. Globalization is another step in that evolution. It is not a unique event just bursting onto the scene, but rather, the 21st century version of a predictable age old dynamic. Yet due to the accelerated pace at which change now occurs, a backlash is growing and supported by a variety of groups.

Just as in nature, if balance is lost, counter forces emerge that push back in an attempt to seek an arrangement that works. For example, when deer populations exceed their environmental limitations, dwindling food supplies reduce their number. This natural countering effect occurs in all systems, including religious, political and economic ones. For example, when overzealous popes wielded excessive power, the Protestant Reformation formed and challenged existing doctrine. When the Great Depression caused unemployment to skyrocket, Fascism emerged as an alternative political system. And, when unrestrained laissez-faire capitalism became the rage, Marxism provided the opposition. Unfortunately, since cause and effect do not always fall closely together, forces often do not or cannot see the unintended consequences of their actions.

Just as there was no halting the Industrial Revolution, globalization will not be stopped. But it can be slowed—and this prospect has the potential to undermine our quality of life. Through misinformation or unbalanced media reports, anti-globalist forces may have reached a tipping point, and through major protests, persuaded millions of people to fear, not embrace, globalization.

The results are obvious. In December 1999, thousands of protesters disrupted the WTO meeting in Seattle. Police fired tear gas and rubber bullets on crowds of activists and the talks ended prematurely. In April 2000, thousands of protesters descended upon a World Bank and International Monetary Fund meeting paralyzing Washington, D.C. In September 2000, Czech police used tear gas and water cannons to prevent demonstrators from closing down a World Bank and International Monetary Fund conference in Prague. In April 2001, anti-globalization activists disrupted a Summit of the Americas meeting in Quebec, Canada. In July 2001, young Italian activists were fatally shot by police in a confrontation at the G8 summit in Genoa, Italy. Although anti-globalist voices have faded since the September 11, 2001 terrorist attacks on the United States, the movement remains strong. The most recent reminder occurred at the July 2005 G8 summit. Reportedly, 3,500 protesters, many shouting anti-globalization slogans amid others who spoke out on African poverty and climate change, marched through the Scottish village of Auchterarder near the Gleneagles Resort, the host of the summit. Several hundred protestors clashed with police. The summit was not overshadowed by protesters, however, but by terrorist bombings in London.

Anti-globalist organizations, whose intentions are admirable, often describe themselves as human rights groups. In response, they achieve a moral high ground and in turn, often get the benefit of the doubt from the press. Ironically, if the policies advocated by these organizations were ever implemented, they would do tremendous damage to the groups they seek to help.

Few organizations have attempted to counter the anti-globalization movement. Corporate America, which has the resources to do so, needs to provide balance and set the record straight. In a May 2005 opinion-editorial (op-ed), Thomas Friedman, author of *The World Is Flat: A Brief History of the Twenty-first Century* and *New York Times* columnist, said "After six weeks of being a foreign correspondent traveling around America, the biggest question I have come home with is not 'What's the matter with Kansas?' but rather, 'What's the matter with big business?' ... when I look around for the group that has both the power and interest in seeing America remain globally focused and competitive—American business leaders—they seem to be missing in action."

In the 1970s and 1980s, Japan was the country most feared by the United States in terms of economic competition. In fact, in the minds of many, the promise of America was over; Japanese economic power would dictate. In the 1990s, Mexico became the focus of the American public. Ross Perot had millions of Americans convinced that we would all hear a "giant sucking sound" as U.S. jobs headed south, a famously incorrect forecast. Now, globalization, China and India have become top of mind in terms of economic threats. Is this justified? Yes, if you believe most of what you read in the newspapers. As a result of these fears and new challenges, companies need to be mindful how they explain the impact of today's fast-moving changes on their businesses—and exceptionally careful about how they communicate what they intend to do about them. Since a large number of Americans, including reporters, policymakers, employees and investors, believe trade and globalization represent forces to fear, not opportunities to seize, crafting messages in this environment of distrust is very difficult. By implementing the strategies detailed in Part II and considering the talking points in Part III, you will be better prepared to achieve your communications goals.

Part II

Tips and Strategies for Communicating Messages

International trade and globalization have been vital factors in the economic growth and wealth creation of the United States. Now, due to current trends, trade and globalization are even more important to our future well-being. In addition to being a primary generator of business and job growth, they also provide consumers greater disposable income, further improving our standard of living. For example, a May 2005 report published by the OECD, says reforms that enhance market competition, reduce tariff barriers and ease restrictions on FDI are estimated to boost GDP per capita 1 to 3 percent in the United States, 2 to 3.5 percent in the European Union, and an average of 1.25 to 3 percent in OECD member countries. But while the gains are widely dispersed, the much smaller losses are highly concentrated. And due to a massive dissemination of mis-information, many believe trade and globalization primarily are responsible for America's economic difficulties. In turn, this has led to the belief that erecting trade barriers will solve a variety of problems. Nothing could be further from the truth.

To reverse these perceptions, American businesses must take the lead in educating the public, media and policymakers, and of course, their employees and investors on today's global economic realities. And very importantly, they must communicate the impact of these realities on their companies and explain what they intend to do about them. But to truly achieve understanding, it is important to frame or position an issue in a context the target audience can easily grasp. For example, when discussing a particular effect of trade, explain it in terms we all value (i.e., our homes and family, career opportunities, wage potential and quality of life). Attempting to discuss issues solely in economic, theoretical or non-emotional terms is likely to result in a lack of understanding or limited engagement on the part of the target audience.

Just as important, it is essential to keep the message simple. To do so, narrowly focus on the goal. Unfortunately, when complex issues are discussed or responses to questions are provided to the media, policymakers, employees or investors, the communicator often attempts to convey too much information—creating confusion and new objections. In the end, the audience may not have the background, possess the necessary level of detail or connect all the dots. And even if the target audience is fully up to speed on every aspect, they may only retain 20 percent of what is expressed. The solution is not to repeat the points five times, but rather, to prioritize your answers with the most concise and compelling information available (see logic train in Part III). Furthermore, keeping the message simple and concise also will allow you to communicate it in little time. And since you are likely to only have a few seconds to convey a compelling argument on radio, television or at a town hall meeting, for example, few alternatives exist. And remember, credibility is key! Manage expectations and do not oversell what is realistically anticipated to occur based on a corporate decision or response to globalization.

Foreign Businesses and Governments Need To Explain Proactively
the Advantages and Disadvantages of Trade Liberalization

The need to more effectively communicate today's economic realities and a sound response also exists outside the United States. In fact, almost every country, especially those that intend to further liberalize trade in Central America, South America and Eastern Europe, must proactively craft messages that honestly explain the short-term downside in context with the much greater upside. Overall, trade liberalization brings tremendous opportunities. But it also brings competition that is likely to hurt inefficient companies in the short term. A communications campaign that explains this, and perhaps is followed up with educational assistance and the implementation of safety nets, will be appreciated by a variety of domestic publics and will go a long way in terms of balancing public opinion.

If a proactive communications campaign is not implemented, stories about small businesses going bankrupt will be repeated in the media. On the other hand, good news about companies signing international contracts and hiring more employees will go unheard. And within a short period of time, the general perception of trade liberalization likely will become negative. In turn, frustration, fear and anger—all based on inaccurate perceptions—will be targeted at policymakers.

The following information will help businesses and governments, both in the United States and abroad, more effectively communicate their actions and policies in order to generate greater understanding and support.

Working with the Media

When dealing with newspapers, magazines, radio and television companies, as well as electronic and online media, it is imperative to understand one key thing: the media is bombarded with information daily. This information comes in numerous forms, such as news releases from companies and community groups, announcements from local, state and federal government agencies, and stories from wire services (i.e. Associated Press International).

This enormous and overwhelming amount of information cannot possibly be covered in the press. So what makes the media select some stories over others? Simply put, reporters like unique, interesting and especially controversial stories that relate to their readers' lives. Unfortunately, quite often the media may be quick to decide that any announcement regarding a company's global business decisions could mean bad news for the public. As a result, when communicating your company's global business decisions, be sure to let reporters know exactly how your decisions will impact your employees and local community. And use the suggested talking points in Part III to help put your company's decisions in context.

However, to ensure the best possible coverage of your company and its position, it is imperative to establish a relationship with the media before any potentially negative information is released. You can do this by suggesting a positive story idea before any difficult decisions are made. But you need to know that today's media works more quickly than ever before. Racing against the clock and competing with instantaneous information channels, the media does not have any time to waste. This is why you must respect the media's time constraints and learn when is the best time to contact a reporter. In general, the best time of day to contact a news desk is early to mid-morning, but many reporters also work evenings. When in doubt, prior to sending any information to the media, call the reporter to introduce yourself and find out what is best for his/her schedule.

Reporters need to grasp the central idea of a story, understand what makes it newsworthy and put it into words and images their readers/viewers can best understand. So overall, the best approach to take with the media is to be honest, up front and sincere. If you consistently tell the plain and simple truth to reporters in the most prompt manner possible—even when the news may be sensitive or controversial—you will help your company beyond compare. And, if you demonstrate respect for a reporter's time, job requirements and position, chances are he/she will treat you in kind.

Media Tips

Once you've created an environment of mutual respect, you may find yourself dealing with the media in a variety of ways, such as through a telephone or in-person interview, at a news conference or public event, or even over a friendly luncheon meeting. To avoid speculation, rumors or negative publicity, and regardless of the situation, ongoing communication with the media should follow some simple steps.

Before an Interview
- Appoint a company spokesperson(s). It may be the CEO, another member of senior management and/or your company's communications expert. Next, make sure this person is well trained and works closely with the company's in-house communications department (or if your company has no in-house expertise, a communications/public relations professional). The appointee should be well-spoken, knowledgeable, confident and able to present the company's viewpoint clearly and coherently, even when under pressure. Using one to two spokespeople will guarantee that your company messages and positions remain consistent and constant.

- Familiarize yourself with the publication or program at which your interviewer is employed. Understanding the reporter's audience, format and context is key.
- Respond promptly to interview requests. It is fine to call a reporter back as soon as possible and then schedule a time to speak a little bit later. Whatever you do, do not ignore calls or forget to call a reporter back. Nothing angers a reporter more than being ignored.
- Always have clear answers to Who? What? When? Where? Why? and How? And be sure your answers are short and quotable.
- Be prepared, know your facts and have printed materials, including background information, charts or photos ready to share. These materials may take the form of a press kit, which also contains your company's history, contact numbers and any other relevant information.
- Create some difficult questions you think might be asked and practice your response. Role play interview situations with another employee until you feel comfortable.
- Videotape your practice sessions and check your body language and eye contact. You should appear calm and focused and you should look at the interviewer, not the camera or off in the distance. In short, it's imperative that you come across confident but not cocky.
- Choose the most important point you want to make and put the following in front of it: "The key thing here is..." No matter what questions are asked, find a way to communicate that one sentence message.
- Work on making your comments brief and not filling in silent pauses or dead air time. It is the reporter's job to keep the interview moving along.
- Think very carefully before turning down an interview request. Refusal to talk with the media can be construed as if you have something to hide. Plus, reporters always will go to another source, and he/she may not be as credible or knowledgeable as you are.

During an Interview

- Be consistently positive about your position. Remember every interview is an opportunity to reach a large audience with your own words and images to present your company in a positive light.
- Tell only what you want the interviewer to know. Take your time and answer questions carefully. Remember, every single thing you say can be printed or used! Going "off the record" is not recommended.
- Be polite, friendly and accommodating, never arrogant or defensive. If you do not know the answer to a question, do not be afraid to say "I don't know" or "I need to check on that." And then be sure to get back to the reporter with that information as quickly as possible.
- Whatever you do, do not lie or massage the truth. Also, do not say "No comment." That will make you appear as if you are hiding something.
- Use simple terms and express yourself concisely. Do not use industry abbreviations or jargon. Remember your audience likely is the general public/community and chances are a reporter may not know very much about your topic. As such, do not assume the reporter has background information.
- Use examples or analogies to outline your message. This tactic can illustrate your point in a way that helps the reporter, and ultimately the public, visualize, understand and identify your position (see the fishermen analogy in Part III).
- Listen to the reporter's questions and answer them as best you can. Also try to weave in as much as possible on your company's position. Have a few 10-second sound bites memorized that you can use comfortably. In short, use questions as a jumping-off point or as an opportunity to expand on your position.
- Avoid answering "What if?" questions. In response to those kinds of questions, reply "I don't want to speculate on that."

- Show your concern if there is a problem and demonstrate what your company is doing to address and remedy the situation.
- Stress the human angle and focus on how communities may ultimately benefit from the action you're taking.
- If the story could be construed as negative, don't provide unnecessary information. Stay focused and only answer the questions you are asked.
- Never insult the reporter by asking to see the story before it goes to print. However, you may say "Let's review my quotes to be sure they're all correct." This is two-fold in its focus: you can clear up any misunderstood or misinterpreted statements and you can get an idea of the angle or direction the reporter is taking with the story.
- Offer to be available for additional questions or clarification.

After an Interview
- If by accident you provided or your company released incorrect information, correct it as soon as possible. Most often, the best way to deal with mistakes is to admit you made them and then help correct them.
- Unless a major or egregious error is made, don't call to complain about a story after it appears or airs. If you do feel the need to call, calmly and politely identify the error and request a correction. Chances are simple human error is to blame and you don't want to destroy a media relationship over an isolated event. Remember, it is more important to keep the relationship positive and respectful than to feel vindicated.
- Do not assume that because your company advertises with the reporter's publication or program that your story will receive preferential treatment or placement. Advertising and news are two totally unrelated areas and reporters dislike it when companies think there is any connection or correlation between the two.
- The media controls the final outcome, not you. You have no input

on the use or placement of your interview or anything else you submit to the media (i.e. news release, op-ed). You must respect the media's position and do your best to present your message in the best way possible.

All in all, how well you work with the media plays an extremely important role in the success or failure of communicating your company's decisions. In summary, remember that the messages and information you provide to the media will help determine what the public thinks and whether or not they will understand and support your position. And also remember, what has been outlined above is only a starting point in terms of media relations. For additional information and more detailed strategies, you should work with your in-house communications executive or an outside professional.

Communicating with Employees and Investors

The news media is not the only group with whom you need to communicate. You also need to keep employees and investors informed and in the loop. And, perhaps the most important thing to remember is that employees and investors should always be informed of decisions and announcements prior to the news media whenever possible. Nothing destroys a company's credibility more quickly than when employees or investors, or even customers, learn about company news from an outside source.

Although many of the same concepts utilized when working with the media apply when communicating with employees and investors, such as being honest and sincere, creating strong relationships, demonstrating mutual respect, understanding the other's point of view and time constraints, and not being afraid to admit you do not know something, there are some differences that exist.

One difference is the way in which you communicate the message and the vehicle you use to share information. While the media primarily depends on interviews, employees and investors usually expect written forms of communication, and on a more frequent basis. For employees, this means you can use your company's internal publication/employee newsletter, intranet or internal email system, employee paychecks or even special home mailings to communicate information and company policies. In the case of investors, who may often be the last to believe that change is necessary, quarterly earnings statements, annual reports and specialized mailings may be used. Just remember that whatever you publish may find its way into the media's hands.

Additional ways to communicate with your employees and investors include through specially designed videos, town meetings with a question and answer format and open forums. But no matter which way you choose to communicate, the most important things to do are keep employees and investors informed, be fully honest to combat the creation of rumors, do not make promises you cannot keep and do your best to outline the positives that will result from your company's decisions. Your audiences may be skeptical or hostile, so it is imperative you remain poised and create an atmosphere of cooperation with a sincere intent to be helpful.

In general, your employees and investors are crucial audiences and you must communicate with them just as vigorously as you do with the media, if not more so. Employees and investors who respect management, take pride in the company's products or services, and believe they are being treated with dignity and respect are imperative to a company's success.

An Example of the Effects of New Global
Realities and Poor Communication

A company well known for its high quality products provides an example that demonstrates the changing face of globalization and the importance of good media and employee communications.

The company in question, referred to here as Company X, dominated its industry for decades. Early in the 20th century, it had factories in New York State, England and Australia. Toward the end of the century, even though it controlled a major share of the North American market, competitors in the Pacific Rim and Europe were growing stronger. To maintain its marketshare, Company X was forced to match its competitors' pricing. But by the 1980s, it could no longer sustain this strategy.

Company X's manufacturing process, which even today does not lend itself to high levels of automation, faced competition from Pacific Rim producers performing assembly in the Philippines and Europeans assembling in Turkey. As a result, the company could not improve productivity enough to erase the wage gap. In an op-ed, Company X's CEO said the firm had a choice: sell out to off-shore interests or move lower-skilled jobs to Mexico. He chose to locate lower-skilled work in Texas and perform assembly in Mexico. He believed this would reduce manufacturing costs and retain well-paid skilled jobs in New York State.

In turn, the manufacturer built world class plants in Texas and Mexico. Consequently, several hundred good jobs were created in a depressed region of Texas, while approximately 1,500 new jobs shifted to desperately poor workers in Mexico—jobs which provided excellent working conditions and paid well above the average Mexican wage. Very important to the company chairman, the manufacturer saved about 1,000 well paying jobs in New York, his home state.

By establishing a plant in Mexico, the firm saved good jobs in the United States that likely would have been lost to Asia. However, according to Bill McKibben, a communications consultant and former communications counsel to the manufacturer, many of the company's New York workers did not see it that way. As a result, morale fell and productivity plunged. Had Company X's workforce accepted the global realities and difficult choices the firm faced, employee rumors may not have become accepted as fact and bad press may have been minimized, McKibben says. When retained by Company X, McKibben was advised not to waste time with the local media. The company's management believed the local media would not fairly represent the manufacturer's efforts. However, after meeting with the media, McKibben was able to put the global realities in context. Thereafter, he continued to keep the media informed and on a factual course. Nevertheless, damage, which played a part in the closing of the New York plant a decade later, had been done.

The manufacturer eventually regained its competitive position and was sold to a larger U.S. firm. Today, the company's headquarters is no longer in New York, and it maintains various facilities both in the United States and around the world. The manufacturer continues to dominate its product category in North America.

This story involved a company scrambling to adapt to its changing business environment while trying to keep good jobs in New York State. Unfortunately, its intentions were not effectively communicated to the media or employees, and this factor played a large role in the eventual closing of its New York factory.

McKibben's Four Media Rules

Bill McKibben offers the following four simple—but not easy to follow—rules to successful public relations:

- *Do the right thing.* Consider more than profit and personal gain. Long term corporate health is based on a happy workforce. In turn, happy employees will make your customers happy, and that combination will make your investors happy.

- *When you are forced to make tough decisions, be proactive.* Consult all involved and see if they have a way to lessen the downside. Be sure everyone knows the choices. Let everyone affected— employees, investors, the community and your customers— know what is being considered and your ultimate or final decision.

- *Make the media your partner.* Connect with them early on. Tell them everything as soon as those closest to the issues are on board. Candor and openness will be rewarded. If there are factors that will help the media understand an issue but would be better not published, ask if you can go off the record. If you establish an atmosphere of trust, you can work with the media and they will work with you.

- *If something bad happens, communicate it immediately.* This is always the hardest part of dealing with the media. If you attempt to hide anything or hold back, the media will speculate and rumor will become accepted as fact. Instead of a day or week of bad press, the media will keep probing while the bad press continues on and on. The classic case is the 1982 Tylenol poisoning tragedy. Faced with seven deaths, Johnson & Johnson never hesitated. The company halted sales and recalled the product. It initiated an internal investigation that indicated the poison could not have been added in its facilities. Johnson & Johnson offered a reward for the capture of the perpetrator and came to the aid of grieving families of the victims. By quickly aligning itself with the victims, Johnson & Johnson also was seen as a victim. Its response to this crime was successful and the company soon regained lost marketshare.

Educating Policymakers via Grassroots Coalitions

In order to prosper well in the 21st century, and seize the benefits and mitigate the dangers presented by globalization, it is imperative for companies to expand internationally. But to do so, it is essential that elected officials do not craft protectionist policies, but instead, pass pro-globalist and trade liberalizing legislation that further opens foreign markets. In order to achieve this, businesses must better educate policymakers on today's global economic realities.

An effective means to achieve this is through the building and managing of grassroots coalitions. To succeed, these coalitions must be well organized, and if possible, able to permanently operate on a national level. When selecting grassroots coalition participants, include employees who share common beliefs and interests. And remember, it is important to include other companies and their employees, as well as influential members of the business community who represent sizable employment. But to achieve a truly broad-based coalition, you must include opinion leaders, political contributors, academics, students, business associations and other organizations who understand the importance of trade and globalization.

To win each policymaker's support, it is important to:

- Publish compelling position papers that support your positions.
- Coordinate meetings between policymakers and coalition members to discuss the positions and the impact on local companies, employees and communities.
- Encourage coalition members to submit op-eds to local newspapers that explain the importance of the positions, and recognize the efforts of policymakers who already have supported them.
- Encourage coalition members to attend newspaper editorial board meetings to explain the positions.
- Generate letter-writing campaigns to encourage policymakers to advance the positions or to thank those who have already supported them.
- Obtain quotes from coalition members expressing the importance of the positions to their companies and workers, and in turn, provide them to policymakers and/or include them in op-eds.
- Educate newspaper reporters on your position in an attempt to generate positive or balanced articles.
- Sponsor educational events that promote the positions.

To ensure success, it is important to provide members of the coalition with talking points, as well as sample drafts of op-eds and "Dear Member of Congress" letters. And in order to get all boats moving upstream together, it is vital to compromise when necessary, focusing on common interests while setting aside differences.

Focus on Congressional Districts

Organizations that advocate anti-globalist policies are gaining strength. And during periods of poor economic growth characterized by rising unemployment, labor unions and other organizations put even greater pressure on Congress to protect poor performing industries. Unfortunately, although well intentioned, this pressure can result in anti-globalist positions that end in fewer, not more American jobs. National coalitions that counter these trends by advocating pro-globalist positions at the Congressional district level are increasingly necessary. Interestingly, national coalitions that operate at the district level also are becoming more effective and have a significant collective impact on the positions of Members of Congress.

As this occurs, the effectiveness of Washington, D.C.-based lobbyists may be declining. Why? Inside the D.C. beltway tens of thousands of lobbyists compete for the attention of policy makers. Distinguishing their messages and the degree of importance each one has on constituents back home is increasingly difficult for policymakers. In turn, D.C.-based lobbyists are finding it harder to acquire the attention of politicians.

For these and other reasons, messages initiated from districts that are championed by political supporters and friends of the policymaker, as well as local employers, are becoming increasingly potent. In turn, Members of Congress appear to be paying greater attention to the positions expressed by their constituents. But this is no surprise. Since "the squeaky wheel gets the grease," labor unions and other groups with anti-globalist agendas are increasingly establishing permanent field teams at the district level to engage in this more "retail" method of advancing political agendas. This personal style of advocacy has grown more practical over the years as Members of Congress seek to have expanded input from their districts rather than rely on "inside the beltway" sources.

Small and medium-size companies, which are impacted by anti-globalist policies, often want to tell their stories to policymakers and the media. But since many small and medium-size company executives wear several hats, little time and few resources are available to devote to issue management or advocacy. As a result, the need for big business or business organizations to build, manage, educate and lead coalitions composed of small businesses, as well as others, is very important.

Experience from the Field

Over the last dozen years or so, this author has managed numerous coalitions, including those established to support passage of the North American Free Trade Agreement (NAFTA), the GATT Uruguay Round Agreements, Fast Track Negotiating Authority, China Most Favored Nation trade status (MFN), China Normal Trade Relations status (NTR), China Permanent Normal Trade Relations status (PNTR), and Trade Promotion Authority (TPA). In the end, the Congressional votes needed were obtained. But it was not easy. It was partly accomplished by educating thousands of members of the business community and other publics as to the benefits of international trade to their companies, employees and communities. In turn, through phone calls and letters sent to Members of Congress, meetings with policymakers and their staffs, op-eds placed in local newspapers, favorable or balanced articles written by reporters, editorial endorsements from editorial-page editors, and countless radio shows, etc., our coalitions confidently expressed their support for the legislation we were seeking.

The result: during a 10 month period, our national media campaign designed to support a particular bill in Congress resulted in 75 op-eds placed, 24 Letters to the Editor placed, 64 editorial board meetings, 56 public/media events, and 25 articles crediting our organization. In addition, during this period our coalition also achieved 384 face-to-face meetings with Members of Congress, 178 face-to-face meetings with Congressional staffers, 30 public forum questions asked, 5,245 letters and faxes sent to Members of Congress, 544 e-mails sent to Members of Congress, 230 phone calls made to Members of Congress, and 745 phone calls made to Congressional staffers.

Additionally, our national coalition distributed 69,411 reports, and worked with the business community to place 84 articles in association mailings and 25 articles in employee newsletters. Our impact was broad and our messages reached numerous policy makers at critical stages in the legislative process. The efforts of our coalition during this campaign resulted in passage of the legislation in the House of Representatives by a margin of almost 55 percent.

Of the 124 Members of Congress targeted by our coalition, 81 voted favorably. This represented 65 percent of Members targeted—a 20 percent higher approval rate over the House vote. And those were among the more difficult legislators to persuade. Of the 57 Republicans targeted, 48 favored the legislation. This represented 84 percent of Republicans targeted. Of the 67 Democrats targeted, 33 favored the legislation. This represented 49 percent. From its modest beginnings in a handful of states, our coalition expanded to include more than two dozen states, and it reached 329 House districts and 50 United States Senators. This represented 76 percent of House Members and 50 percent of Senators.

Communicating in Foreign Markets

There are notable cultural differences among reporters in Manhattan, Silicon Valley and Houston. Consequently, effectively dealing with them requires a degree of cultural sensitivity. Now, add an international layer to the mix. For U.S. business people seeking favorable public opinion in markets outside the United States, it is essential to research and respect the culture of the foreign media, employees, investors and policymakers. In the end, how well you understand their culture and demonstrate your knowledge of what is and is not appropriate will have a major impact on your relationship and its ability to produce favorable results.

Defined as a society's collection of values, beliefs, behaviors, customs and attitudes, culture is also often chock full of nuances that cannot always be explained. Culture is learned, embedded and interrelated. In addition, it defines individual and group similarities and differences. But no matter what, culture cannot be ignored. America—the melting pot of the 20th and 21st centuries—embraces cultural diversity. Yet, the land of plenty may not always be the first to acknowledge the foreign media's culture. The result: a poor relationship from the beginning.

Chances are you are familiar with the expression "When in Rome, do as the Romans do." As children, we are taught to do what is asked of us in terms of dinner and bedtime rituals when staying at a friend's house. Yet, sometimes when children become adults this valuable lesson is forgotten and hurts the ability to forge new relationships. Attitudes and societal values differ considerably throughout the world and this needs to be recognized. For example, acceptable behavior in one cultural setting may be viewed as immoral, unethical or rude in another. Take for instance, kickbacks. While often expected in some countries, these extras may land one in jail in other parts of the world. And nepotism, while prevalent in some corners of the globe, is frowned upon in others. Levels of product support and expectations of consumer loyalty also vary. For example, in the United States a limited warranty often is considered generous. In Japan, even when the warranty expires, the seller still is expected to support the product to some extent. Being familiar with cultural norms will help eliminate misunderstandings.

Many cultures also regard time and status as very different commodities. For example, Germans tend to be extremely time conscious and highly punctual. On the other hand, Latin Americans and Italians tend to have a more relaxed sense of time. This means a German reporter may arrive 15 minutes early for an appointment, while a Latin American may arrive 15 to 30 minutes late. If one is not familiar with the different ways these cultures view time, a problem could arise. For example, one could erroneously assume that the Italian reporter values the meeting less than the German reporter.

Employee work standards or ethics in other cultures also vary. In general, U.S. and German business people are considered driven and hard hitting. Yet, this could lead Mexicans to feel slighted since little time is allocated to friendship development—something Mexicans value. Americans typically prefer to get right down to business after a few minutes of small talk. To some, this does not support friendship—a prerequisite to building a mutually beneficial relationship in many countries. In Saudi Arabia, for example, an initial investor meeting may be designed to establish mutual trust. As such, business usually is not even discussed until the second meeting.

For those doing business in Japan, it is key to know that Japanese culture is defined in hierarchical terms with the good of the group reigning supreme. In this culture, emphasis is placed on seniority and group well-being instead of youth or individual performance. As a result, seeking a decision from an investor without a group consensus, for example, is extremely difficult and could just as well shatter a deal. Similarly, status, which can be identified by titles on business cards, carries much weight across the Asian continent. When deciding to whom one should speak or determining the level of formality to use when speaking, definitely consider the status of your foreign contact. In general, it is better to be more formal than less formal.

Cultural practices also play a large role in determining national strengths. For example, most product development in Asia is performed by entry-level personnel. Once promoted, this work usually is passed into the hands of new inexperienced arrivals. In the United States, when technical product development personnel are promoted, they frequently retain their technical functions instead of moving into management positions. U.S. companies also encourage dissent and the questioning of common practices. These cultural practices often lead to thinking "outside the box" and contribute to American inventiveness and ingenuity. In Japan, as noted above, decisions are usually based on consensus. This practice is known for advancing strong iterative skills that result in valuable product refinement.

Many nations also have specific customs worth noting. In India, for instance, the right hand should be used for eating, giving and accepting since the left hand is considered unclean. Pointing with the index finger is considered impolite in Malaysia; it is more appropriate to point with the thumb of the right hand with the fingers folded under. Furthermore, in France, a firm, vigorous handshake is considered uncultured. And, in the Middle East, one should not point one's finger at someone or show the soles of one's feet when seated. Foot soles are considered unclean and offensive.

Nonverbal communication also plays a very important part of any relationship, especially since the meaning behind gestures and facial expressions can vary significantly. For example, nodding "yes" in the U.S. is equivalent to "no" in Bulgaria. It should come as no surprise to an astute business person that body posture, positioning and eye contact are equivalent to "reading between the lines" and usually influence how one is perceived. Take for instance the following example: the joining of the thumb and forefinger in a circle while extending the other three fingers symbolizes "OK" in the U.S. However, in Malta, this symbol signifies homosexuality; in Japan, money; in France, inadequacy; and in many parts of Eastern Europe, vulgarity.

In some cultures, an employee may sometimes say yes when asked about his ability and willingness to complete a task even when he has no intention of doing so. Why? In the employee's eyes, saying no to a manager may be considered disrespectful or rude. Or, the employee may feel compelled to say yes for fear of losing face. In these cases, the employee would rather lie than seem incapable of performance. In the U.S., yes almost always means yes. The American business world does not leave much room for shades of gray. As a result, understanding the motive behind a yes that actually means no could help improve a deteriorating relationship.

One typical obstacle to building a successful international business relationship is ethnocentric behavior. Unfortunately, Americans sometimes are perceived as arrogant with little willingness to accept or adapt to the foreign culture, including communicating in the host country's language. When U.S. firms establish foreign subsidiaries, some tend to implement a communications policy of "one size fits all," and don't always consider different cultural modes of doing business. This ethnocentric behavior is often regarded by foreign media, as well as employees, investors and policymakers, as rude and disrespectful. In turn, miscommunications can lead to missed opportunities.

To counter this behavior, it is extremely important for U.S. business people to speak the host country's language whenever possible. Even simply attempting to communicate in the host country's native tongue can work wonders in demonstrating mutual respect and a willingness to build trust.

U.S. corporations operating in foreign countries often act as agents of change, bringing improved operating standards, cutting-edge technology and best business practices. But because change sometimes causes anxiety and fear, it is not always welcome—regardless of the benefits. Not being culturally sensitive can certainly begin with bad press and end in lost deals. On the other hand, a sound understanding and respect of foreign cultures can help you satisfy your international communications objectives and achieve your corporate goals.

Part III

Frequently Asked Questions and Talking Points

There are a multitude of frequently asked questions (FAQs) by the media, policymakers, employees and investors about globalization, its impact and how companies plan to respond. Unfortunately, the answers provided by business executives, as well as those in corporate communications departments, often result in more, sometimes hostile questions. Why? Those communicating the answers often do not put them in the appropriate context and/or do not have a sound understanding of today's global issues. As a result, the answers usually create new objections, are muddled, complex, confusing and sometimes appear to be purposefully evasive. This quickly creates an atmosphere of distrust. The result: negative publicity that in some cases has destroyed businesses.

In order to effectively respond to sensitive issues that could impact the interests of a company or organization, it is essential to have an adequate understanding of the subject, its leverage points, emotional hot buttons, likely objections and the talking points required to successfully overcome those objections.

In determining how to address various issues, proceed with a process this author describes as riding the "logic train." In discussing the dimensions of a particular topic, a flow of logic may drive the train in a particular direction. After more debate, an important point or obstacle may turn the train in another direction. And after even more deliberation, the train may turn on a totally different track. The benefits of this analysis are tremendous. In addition to considering a variety of perspectives, the experience of riding the logic train reveals a multitude of issues not initially considered relevant. In the end, by looking at a topic from 360 degrees, you will be prepared to confidently and persuasively discuss the most controversial issues. This may be tantamount to playing chess—with a focus on the next four moves.

What follows are frequently asked questions involving sensitive international business issues and their coinciding compelling talking points. But to achieve greater depth and perhaps more appropriate responses—which requires an understanding of situational details—riding the logic train and applying strategies outlined in Part II are highly recommended.

Developing Countries

FAQ: Do U.S. manufacturers who establish facilities abroad typically seek cheap labor, provide poor working conditions and welcome lax environmental laws?

Talking Points:

Although U.S. manufacturers are anticipated to invest an increasing amount of capital in China over the next decade, overall, only a relatively small portion of U.S. FDI is invested in developing countries or countries with low-cost labor. Contrary to what many believe, in 2003 only 15 percent of U.S. manufacturing FDI was directed into developing countries, including China, according to the Deloitte research report, *Growing the Global Corporation: Global Investment Trends of U.S. Manufacturers.* This number is up from 7 percent in 2002, but down from 22 percent in 2001, 25 percent in 2000, and 32 percent in 1999.

"Despite what would appear to be major opportunities for FDI in emerging markets, such as China and India, most U.S. manufacturers are putting their investment bets on the developed markets... For example, U.S. manufacturing FDI into India fell to just over $50 million in 2003, down 80 percent from nearly $250 million in 1999. Investments by U.S. manufacturers into China—a hotbed of global manufacturing expansion—reached $760 million in 2003; down more than 52 percent from nearly $1.3 billion in 1999, although recovering slightly from a low of $575 million in 2002," the Deloitte report said.

The most important determinants of capital flows are political stability, education and productivity levels, communications and transportation infrastructure, the rule of law, proximity to market and the ability to repatriate profits. This is why developed countries, which pay the highest wages and have the strongest environmental laws, are the destinations for the vast majority of foreign direct investment. This also is why foreign companies operate in the United States—companies that employed 5.4 million Americans with a U.S. payroll of $307 billion in 2002.

Although exceptions exist, many anti-globalist organizations would have you believe that, as a whole, U.S. manufacturers investing abroad seek low-cost facilities that provide sweatshop-like working conditions. If this were correct, investment would be flowing to underdeveloped countries with the poorest labor standards and environmental records. In reality, as demonstrated above, the opposite is true. Although the intentions of these anti-globalist organizations are good, their logic is flawed.

American manufacturers who do invest in developing countries typically offer higher wages and better working conditions than local employers. This makes jobs at U.S. facilities highly prized and, over time, leads to improved environmental and worker protection at all levels. In fact, U.S. companies operating abroad act as agents for change. Through their operating standards, business practices, values and principles, U.S. companies often serve as role models, charting a path for other foreign and domestic companies to follow. This strategy, which is good for business, results in greater employee loyalty, less absenteeism, higher morale and increased productivity.

Procter & Gamble is a case in point. From 1991 through 2002, the company invested $85 million in a Czech Republic consumer products company that produces detergent and liquid cleaners. By applying P & G's worldwide environmental standards, the facility was able to reduce boiler emissions by 99 percent and solid waste by nearly 6,000 metric tons. In addition to environmental improvements, P & G introduced a competitive compensation program and unique employee benefits, such as loans to renovate apartments and houses, supplementary income payments during illness, maternity leave, and language studies. In 2002, it was reported that P & G also donated $120,000 annually to the development of local education, health care, environmental protection, and social institutions. So impressed with these practices, Czech Republic former President Vaclav Havel recently said P & G "could serve as a model for other investors."

Other American corporations investing in facilities abroad typically promote similar ethical and responsible behaviors. Reported in 2002, Nike, the Oregon athletic attire and shoemaker, paid about double the prevailing wage at its contract factories throughout Southeast Asia and scrupulously met all local environmental and occupational safety and health laws.

Studies show that after a country's per capita income reaches about $5,000, environmental improvement becomes a higher national priority. Why? As living standards rise, the population becomes better educated, more politically aware and sophisticated. In turn, greater pressure is put on government to establish and enforce stricter environmental regulations and allocate more resources to environmental quality. And, as incomes rise, more families can afford to send their children to school rather than to work. Thus, research indicates that child labor declines sharply as the level of economic development increases. Many forget that the United States and every other developed nation followed this path.

FAQ: Have trade and globalization harmed developing countries or the poor?

Talking Points:

From 1970 through 2001, world infant mortality rates decreased by almost half, adult literacy increased more than a third, primary school enrollment rose and the average life span shot up 11 years. And from 1990 through 2002, the number of people in low and middle income countries with access to improved water sources and sanitation facilities also increased, according to the World Bank. Looking forward, from 2002 through 2025, worldwide life expectancy is projected to rise from 64 years to 69 years, and from 62 to 68 in less developed countries, according to the U.S. Census Bureau.

Progress also has been made in reducing poverty. For example, in the short span of 1990 through 1998, the number of people living in extreme poverty in East Asia and the Pacific decreased 41 percent—one of the largest and most rapid reductions in history. And between 1990 and 1999, the average proportion of people in developing countries living on less than a dollar per day fell from 32 percent to 25 percent, the World Bank says.

Today, 24 developing countries representing about 3 billion people, including China, India and Mexico, have adopted policies enabling their citizens to take advantage of globalization. The result: their economies are catching up with rich ones. Over the last two decades ending in the late 1990s, these 24 countries, the World Bank indicates, achieved higher growth in incomes, longer life expectancy and better schooling. During this period, the incomes of the least globalized countries, including Iran, Pakistan and North Korea, dropped or remained static. What distinguishes the fastest growing developing countries from the slowest growing developing countries is clear: their openness to trade.

For many of the world's poorest countries, the primary problem is their inability to participate in the globalization process. Contrary to anti-globalist doctrine, globalization benefits poor nations and the less privileged, as well as wealthy nations and the affluent. According to the 2000 WTO report *Trade, Income Disparity and Poverty,* "Trade liberalization (the removal of trade barriers) helps poor countries catch up with rich ones... this faster economic growth helps to alleviate poverty." In fact, the report concludes, trade "is essential if poor people are to have any hope of a brighter future."

The WTO study concurs with the World Bank report *Growth Is Good for the Poor.* Studying data from 80 countries over four decades, *Growth Is Good for the Poor* confirms that "Openness to foreign trade benefits the poor to the same extent that it benefits the whole economy." *Globalization, Poverty and Inequality,* published in 2000 by the Progressive Policy Institute, contends that "less globalization is generally associated with less development." Similar to other studies, the report concludes that anti-globalists are wrong.

According to this report, "No country has managed to lift itself out of poverty without integrating into the global economy." And who would know this better than former Mexican President Ernesto Zedillo, who said: "In every case where a poor nation has significantly overcome its poverty, this has been achieved while engaging in production for export markets and opening itself to the influx of foreign goods, investment and technology—that is, by participating in globalization." Even former sociologist Fernando Henrique Cardoso, who spoke out against aspects of global dependence, promoted—not resisted—globalization as president of Brazil.

Similar conclusions have been reached by Jeffrey Sachs and Andrew Warner of Harvard University. They contend in their report *Economic Convergence and Economic Policies,* published by the National Bureau of Economic Research, that developing countries with open economies grew by 4.5 percent a year in the 1970s and 1980s, while those with closed economies grew by 0.7 percent a year.

At this rate, open economies double in size every 16 years, while closed economies double every 100 years.

If remaining world merchandise trade barriers are eliminated, potential gains are estimated at $250 to $650 billion annually, according to the International Monetary Fund and World Bank. About one-third to one-half of these gains would accrue in developing countries. Removal of agricultural supports would raise global economic welfare by an additional $128 billion annually, with some $30 billion going to developing countries.

"Globalization has helped reduce poverty in a large number of developing countries but it must be harnessed better to help the world's poorest, most marginalized countries improve the lives of their citizens," states the 2002 World Bank report, *Globalization, Growth and Poverty: Building an Inclusive World Economy.* "This is especially important in the wake of September 11," the World Bank says.

Globalization may not be a panacea for all economic ills, but it certainly helps alleviate them. However, it has had negative consequences on some developing countries with distorted economies or a lack of sound legal or financial systems. As a result, antiglobalists with good intentions but bad policy recommendations often make globalization the scapegoat for many of the world's problems.

In the end, the facts don't lie. According to authors John Micklethwait and Adrian Wooldridge, "In 1960, the average wage in developing countries was just 10 percent of the average manufacturing wage in the United States; in 1992, despite all that terrible globalization, it had risen to 30 percent... globalization helps the whole pie get bigger." In fact, there are numerous examples of this principle. As stated by Micklethwait and Wooldridge, "Deng Xiaoping's decision to open China's economy in 1978 helped some 800 million peasants more than double their real incomes in just six years, arguably the single greatest leap out of acute poverty of all time."

FAQ: Is there a relationship between globalization and terrorism?

Talking Points:

Yes, but for the opposite reasons many would expect. Stated above, the primary economic problem poor countries incur is not too much globalization, but instead, their inability to participate in it. Take the Middle East for example. It is replete with totalitarian regimes that use trade barriers to isolate themselves from the world, as well as each other. This has resulted in virtually no economic growth in the Middle East and North Africa since 1965. In addition, from 1980 through 2002, the Middle East's share of world trade and investment, excluding Israel, fell by about 75 percent.

Why does global integration hold such promise for the Middle East? Look at the facts. East Asia and the Pacific, a region that has welcomed global integration, generated an average annual growth rate of 5.6 percent from 1965 through the end of the century, and 7.5 percent throughout the 1990s. Plus, in the short span of 1990 through 1998, the number of people living in extreme poverty there decreased 41 percent—one of the largest and most rapid reductions in history.

If free market reform—which is promoted by globalization—is accepted in the Middle East, the region will be positioned to absorb new ideas, technologies and a myriad of other benefits from the world trading community. This will help the region diversify its exports toward agricultural goods and higher-value manufactured products, and in turn, create new jobs. Furthermore, the U.S.-Jordan Free Trade Agreement, signed in 2001, will continue to serve as a model for economic integration for the entire region. Importantly, it will foster the development of a fair and impartial legal system as well as strengthen democratic institutions.

The Middle East would be well advised to adopt free market policies that globalization—which has lifted millions out of poverty—

promotes. As trade and investment increase, the incomes of ordinary people also will rise. This will lead to higher living standards and a better-educated and politically-involved population. In turn, despair and hopelessness, characteristics commonly found among terrorists or their supporters, will slowly turn to hope.

Thomas Barnett, senior strategic researcher at the U.S. Naval War College and author of *The Pentagon's New Map: War and Peace in the Twenty First Century*, says that if we map out U.S. military responses since the end of the Cold War, we find an overwhelming concentration of activity in the regions of the world that are excluded from globalization's core. Barnett argues that regions or countries isolated from globalization or lacking economic and cultural connectivity with the rest of the world are those countries where you will find instability, threats to the international system and terrorist networks. As a result, Barnett notes that the U.S. military shut down roughly 150 military bases in the United States, Europe and developed Asia and established new ones near the non-integrating countries.

Manufacturing and Jobs

FAQ: How is globalization impacting U.S. manufacturing?

Talking Points:

The integration of traditional manufacturing, new technologies, national markets and improved supply chain management—all spawned by globalization—is transforming American manufacturing. In the process, resources have shifted to sectors with competitive advantages. As a result, productivity has climbed to new highs, and due to the American ability to change and improve, innovation is flourishing. For instance, the use of muscle on the factory floor is a thing of the past. Today, self-directed workers operate in teams and apply more sophisticated skills to create and run new processes. Concurrently, competitive forces unleashed by globalization are forcing U.S. manufacturers to compete less on price and focus more on product design, branding strategies, productivity, flexibility, quality and responsiveness to customer needs. And companies must continue to push the envelope in terms of greater specialization.

Thomas Friedman writes in *The Lexus and the Olive Tree* that "The relative decline of the United States in the 1980s was part of America's preparing itself for and adjusting to the new globalization system." This process will continue. With the fast-paced changes brought on by the dynamic global economy, tremendous pressure is put on companies to adapt. Lester Thurow, author and Massachusetts Institute of Technology professor, states that "businesses must be willing to destroy the old while it is still successful if they wish to build the new that will become successful." He points out that makers of vacuum tubes never successfully made transistors after transistors replaced vacuum tubes.

Of the 500 companies that originally comprised the S&P 500 in 1957, only 339 exist today, and this includes descendants of mergers and acquisitions and spin-offs, according to Wharton professor and author Jeremy Siegel. Why? Arie de Geus, author of *The Living Company*, says "The average life expectancy of a multinational corporation—Fortune 500 or its equivalent—is between 40 and 50 years." Long-lived companies, he contends, are sensitive to their environment, cohesive with a strong sense of identity, tolerant and conservative in their financing. But today, it is essential that companies become truly global in order to succeed well into the future.

FAQ: What change does globalization create in the workforce?

Talking Points:

Globalization is forcing ongoing changes similar to those introduced by the industrial revolution. Shifting from an agrarian society to an industrial economy compelled workers to leave farms in search of factory jobs. Industrialization created anxiety and fear and demanded that workers learn new skills. With the advent of globalization, the U.S. is increasingly specializing in more complex, value-added goods and services. Consequently, new skills again are demanded. Gradually, globalization has created, transformed and streamlined jobs in the United States. This has forced workers to continually improve their job skills and add greater value.

But adapting to change is never easy. To help workers adjust to the changing environment, on August 6, 2002, Congress re-authorized the Trade Adjustment Assistance (TAA) program through fiscal year 2007 and added provisions. Overall, the TAA's goal is to help trade-affected workers return to suitable employment as quickly as possible.

Today, the ability to seize the best job opportunities is often dependent on the level of education one has obtained. The occupational groups projected to decline or be among the slowest growing are more likely to be dominated by workers who do not obtain education beyond high school. Conversely, occupations with the highest rates of growth are more likely to employ workers with higher educational attainment.

According to the U.S. Department of Labor's report *Futurework,* "We are living in a new economy—powered by technology, fueled by information, and driven by opportunity on our side." By 2050, the report indicates, the U.S. population is expected to increase by 50 percent. As the knowledge economy emerges, it is essential that our young people develop the skills needed for tomorrow. According to the National Association of Manufacturers, intense competition from the globalization of the manufacturing marketplace, changing demographics and the relentless advancement of technology has challenged U.S manufacturing. "The result has been a dramatic increase in the sector's need for highly skilled, technically savvy employees who can fully exploit the productive potential of advanced technologies and support increased quality and product complexity."

It is very clear: as globalization creates opportunity, it generates more opportunities for those workers who are better educated. Because the uneducated could be left behind, lifelong learning policies are essential in today's economy and even more so in tomorrow's. It is also very important for companies to nurture a proactive global corporate culture that supports these goals.

FAQ: Why are manufacturing jobs declining?

Talking Points:

The number of U.S. manufacturing jobs declined from a high of 21 million in 1979 to 14.3 million in June 2005. During this period, the percentage of manufacturing jobs relative to total U.S. employment fell from 21 percent to about 10 percent. The primary reason: a combination of technology and high productivity. Productivity gains generated by new technologies in manufacturing have consistently outpaced productivity gains in other sectors of the economy. As a result, new technologies and processes have permitted manufacturing firms to produce ever-increasing output with fewer higher paid workers.

According to Federal Reserve Governor Ben Bernanke, "In real terms, manufacturing production in the United States has risen rapidly over the last fifty years... If manufacturing output has not declined, then what explains the sharp reductions in U.S. manufacturing employment that have occurred not only in the past few years but over preceding decades as well? The answer is a stellar record of productivity growth. Over the years, new technologies, processes and products have permitted manufacturing firms to produce ever-increasing output with ever fewer workers. The long-run trend in manufacturing is similar to what occurred earlier in agriculture." Bernanke also notes, "Strong productivity growth provides major benefits to the U.S. economy in the long term, including higher real incomes and more efficient and competitive industries."

FAQ: Is the U.S. economy able to produce new jobs to compensate for those lost in manufacturing?

Talking Points:

Yes. The U.S. economy generated 60 million net new jobs from 1970-2000, and is predicted to create another 21.3 million net jobs from 2002 through 2012, according to the U.S. Department of Labor, Bureau of Labor Statistics. Daniel Hecker, an economist in the Office of Occupational Statistics and Employment Projections, Bureau of Labor Statistics, says, "The economy will continue generating jobs for workers at all levels of education and training, although growth rates are projected to be faster, on average, for occupations generally requiring a postsecondary award (a vocational certificate or other award or an associate or higher degree) than for occupations requiring less education or training. Most new jobs, however, will arise in occupations that require only work-related training (on-the-job training or work experience in a related occupation), even though these occupations are projected to grow more slowly, on average."

Job losses, often erroneously assumed to be the result of international trade and globalization, are frequently reported in the media. Unfortunately, job gains are rarely covered in newspapers or on television, and therefore, not recognized by the general public. The bad news, which has had a cumulative negative effect on public opinion, is clearly revealed in public surveys.

Services

FAQ: What impact do service exports have on the economy and jobs?

Talking Points:

For over three decades, the U.S. service sector has generated a trade surplus that has consistently reduced the trade deficit. For example, in 2004, U.S. services exports of $338.6 billion decreased the U.S. trade deficit by almost $50 billion, and the service export figure is probably severely underreported. Since 1980, U.S. service exports have grown almost twice as quickly as goods exports.

But more importantly, tremendous benefits are currently derived from—and huge potential is offered by—the service sector in terms of economic growth, personal income, employment and exports. This fact is not widely acknowledged. It is becoming increasingly likely that the telecommunications/digital infrastructure that is making the global sourcing of services possible today is the same infrastructure that will significantly support an even greater boost in service exports.

U.S. Service and Merchandise Exports, in Billions

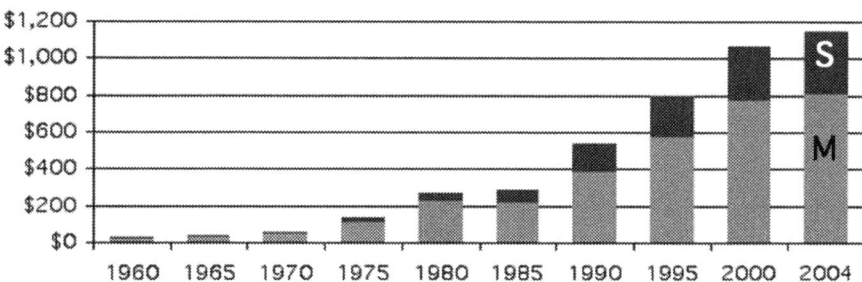

Source: U.S. Department of Commerce

Major U.S. service exports include computer and data processing; wholesale, financial, transportation and communication services; architectural, engineering and surveying services; accounting, research and management services; and motion pictures. And it is anticipated that the export of business, professional and technical services (accounting, advertising, engineering, franchising, consulting, public relations, testing and training) will increase rapidly over the next several years.

When the delivery of services requires face-to-face contact, it is necessary to be present in the foreign market. To accomplish this, many U.S. companies sell their services through U.S.-owned foreign affiliates. U.S.-owned employment agencies operating in Europe, for example, interview hundreds of European candidates each day for local jobs. U.S.-owned insurance affiliates operating abroad, a fast-growing industry, account for a very large share of total U.S.-owned affiliate transactions.

FAQ: Do service jobs pay poorly?

Talking Points:

When some people envision the service sector, they think of employees flipping hamburgers. In reality, the U.S. service sector has become extremely advanced and internationally competitive. In turn, the sector's wages have risen considerably. For example, in December 2002, January 2003 and February 2003, average hourly earnings for service production workers reached $15.49, $15.51 and $15.65, respectively, according to the Bureau of Labor Statistics. During these same months, average hourly earnings for U.S. manufacturing production workers were $15.48, $15.53 and $15.56. This indicates that hourly wages in the service sector have clearly caught up to the manufacturing sector.

With the recent introduction and availability of new and inexpensive technology—led by telecommunications, computers and the internet—millions of people and companies worldwide now have the ability to purchase more services from the United States. As a result, the U.S. service sector will continue to grow. Note: the number of workers employed in U.S. service producing industries has steadily climbed. In June 2005, it reached 111.4 million or 83.4 percent of total payroll employment.

Imports

FAQ: Do imports put U.S. jobs at risk?

Talking Points:

International trade sometimes does cause employment to increase in one sector and decrease in another. But so do many other factors. Exaggerated fears of massive job losses due to imports are misplaced. Contrary to some claims, only a very small percentage of American jobs are ever put at risk from imports. And surprising to many, U.S. employment has been strong during periods of elevated imports.

Stated by the Progressive Policy Institute in June 2005, "What role do trade and the global economy play in job loss? Perhaps less than many people assume. Definitions of 'trade-related' job loss are unclear, reliable statistics are scarce, and the statistics which do emerge are rarely put in the context of total layoffs. But research seems to show that at most they account for about 5 percent of layoffs, and more likely between 2 percent and 3 percent."

According to the Bureau of Labor Statistics payroll data, which does not include farm workers and some self-employed workers, in June 2005 goods-producing industries (manufacturing, mining, logging and construction) accounted for 22 million workers; service-providing industries accounted for the remaining 111 million workers. The workers not in the manufacturing sector are in industries that by their nature do not produce tradable goods or services, or where imports account for a very small to nonexistent share of domestic supply, according to Daniel Griswold, director of the CATO Institute's Center for Trade Policy Studies. And in the manufacturing sector, only a small number of workers are in industries considered import-sensitive.

In 2004, agricultural workers numbered 2.2 million and represented approximately 1.6 percent of total U.S. employment, as reported by the U.S. Department of Labor. According to Griswold, some agricultural sectors (such as dairy products, sugar and peanuts) are more vulnerable than others (the larger export-oriented sectors such as wheat, corn and soybeans). "Even in farm sectors most vulnerable to import competition," said Griswold, "the potential job losses are minuscule in relation to the overall U.S. labor force."

FAQ: What is the impact of imports on consumers?

Talking Points:

Contrary to some claims, imports are good for the economy and consumers. Imports offer American consumers greater choices, a wider range of quality and access to lower-cost goods and services. They create competition, forcing domestic producers to improve value by increasing quality and/or by reducing costs. And since imports allow the American family to purchase more goods for less money—stretching the dollar—more disposable income is available for education, health care, mortgages, vacations, etc. Imports also help keep inflation down, which is one of the most important factors in raising our standard of living.

"Three out of four families living below the poverty line in America today own a washing machine and at least one car," observe John Micklethwait and Adrian Wooldridge, authors of *A Future Perfect*. "Ninety-seven percent own a television; three out of four have a VCR. Thanks to all that terrible competition, many gadgets are much more affordable, particularly in terms of the number of work hours needed to acquire them."

FAQ: Do imports hurt U.S. manufacturers?

Talking Points:

Imports not only afford American families a higher standard of living—a primary economic goal—but through the availability of lower-cost imported components and materials, U.S. producers are more competitive, which result in enormous benefits.

In 2004, more than half the $1.47 trillion in goods Americans imported were capital goods ($344 billion) and industrial supplies and materials ($412 billion). As stated by Daniel Griswold: "Such imports as petroleum, raw materials, steel and semiconductors are used directly by American producers to lower the cost of their final products. The lower costs in turn lead to increased sales at home and abroad, and in many cases, higher employment within the industry."

According to the WTO, "Imports expand the range of final products and services that are made by domestic producers by increasing the range of technologies they can use. When mobile telephone equipment became available, services sprang up even in the countries that did not make the equipment. Additionally, because imports offer unique capabilities at attractive prices, they are proven to enhance worker productivity. And higher productivity leads to a host of benefits."

U.S. Imports in 2004, in Billions

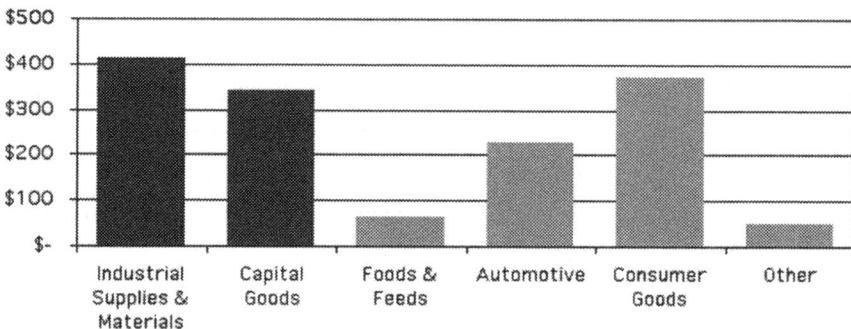

Source: U.S. Department of Commerce

Trade and Investment

FAQ: How important is international trade to the U.S. economy?

Talking Points:

International trade enables producers of goods and services to move beyond the U.S. market of 296 million people and sell to the world market of 6.4 billion. This is very good news, since exports support millions of higher-paying U.S. jobs, strengthen companies and farms, and improve our tax base, while sending export revenue to local communities through restaurants, retail stores, etc. In 1950, trade accounted for less than 5.5 percent of U.S. economic growth. Today, it has become an integral part of everyday life, accounting for 25 percent of economic growth in 2004.

As stated earlier, in 2005 Gary Clyde Hufbauer of the Institute for International Economics, said trade and globalization have generated an increase in U.S. income of approximately $1 trillion annually, measured in 2003 dollars. This translates into an income gain of about $10,000 for the average American household per year. Further liberalization that achieves global free trade and investment, he said, could produce another $500 billion in U.S. income annually or $5,000 per household each year. And a May 2005 OECD report estimates reforms that enhance market competition, reduce tariff barriers and ease restrictions on FDI would boost GDP per capita 1 to 3 percent in the United States, 2 to 3.5 percent in the European Union, and an average of 1.25 to 3 percent in OECD member countries.

According to Howard Lewis III and J. David Richardson's report *Why Global Commitment Really Matters!*, companies that export grow faster and fail less often than companies that do not. And their workers and communities are better off. According to this report, published in October 2001 by the Institute for International Economics, U.S. exporting firms experience 2 to 4 percentage points faster annual growth in employment than their non-exporting counterparts.

But there's more to the story. Exporting firms also offer better opportunities for advancement, expand their annual total sales about 0.6 to 1.3 percent faster, and are nearly 8.5 percent less likely to go out of business. These gains are not dependent on any specific time period or export volume. Furthermore, sales abroad spread risk should the domestic market enter a period of slow growth or recession.

FAQ: Are workers in trade-related jobs paid less than the average wage?

Talking Points:

According to *Why Global Commitment Really Matters!*, workers employed in exporting firms have better-paying jobs. For example, blue-collar worker earnings in exporting firms are 13 percent higher than those in non-exporting plants. Wages are 23 percent higher when comparing large plants and 9 percent higher when comparing small plants. White-collar employees also earn more—18 percent more than their non-exporting counterparts. Furthermore, the benefits for all workers at exporting plants are 37 percent higher and include improved medical insurance and paid leave.

Why Exports Matter: More!, a report by J. David Richardson and Karin Rindal published by the Institute for International Economics and The Manufacturers Institute, states that less skilled workers also earn more at exporting plants. How does globalization impact the wages of workers in non-trade related jobs? According to the International Monetary Fund, "Nearly all research finds only a modest effect of international trade on wages and income inequality." Note: since the late 1970s, the wages of less skilled American workers have decreased relative to those of more skilled workers. Similar patterns are occurring in the United Kingdom. In contrast, countries with relatively rigid wages, such as France, Germany and Italy, have experienced higher unemployment rates.

FAQ: How do U.S. companies that invest abroad or are recipients for foreign direct investment compare with firms not internationally involved?

Talking Points:

According to Lewis and Richardson's report, U.S. companies that have investments abroad use more advanced manufacturing technology than U.S. non-multinationals or U.S. firms without investments abroad. And this has led to greater labor productivity. In fact, worker productivity is 11 percent higher in large U.S. multinationals and 33 percent higher in small ones as compared to their U.S. counterparts not invested abroad.

In addition, average annual earnings of employees at large U.S. multinationals abroad are 18 percent higher than at their U.S. non-multinational counterparts; at small multinationals this number increases to 25 percent. Even though analysis indicates difficulty in separating out white-collar job gains at American-owned multinationals, blue-collar job gains are significant.

On the other hand, U.S companies that are recipients of foreign direct investment also perform better. According to the report, U.S. plants that are recipients of foreign direct investment employ workers with 19 percent higher productivity, provide them with more machinery and equipment, and use more cutting-edge technology than their counterparts not globally engaged. Also noteworthy, these benefits accrue at plants with an equity stake as low as 10 percent and as high as 100 percent. Overall, the report says blue- and white-collar jobs at these plants pay 7 and 2.5 percent more, respectively, when comparing plant size, industry and location.

Production Sharing and Sourcing

FAQ: Do U.S. production sharing operations abroad destroy U.S. jobs?

Talking Points:

Several anti-globalist groups feel U.S. production sharing (the allocation of different stages of the manufacturing process to different countries) is totally unnecessary and should be eliminated. What they don't understand is that production sharing actually saves more jobs here at home than would be lost due to protectionist efforts to place a straight jacket on business.

Production sharing has many benefits. For one, it can result in lower manufacturing costs while increasing a company's level of global competitiveness. This process not only helps retain jobs that otherwise would be lost due to competition, it also grows jobs in capital-intensive manufacturing, product development, design and marketing-related activities here in the U.S.

Also known as co-production or cross-border manufacturing, production sharing allows firms anywhere in the world to comple- ment their respective strengths by providing access to unique tech- nology, raw materials, specialized intermediate inputs or labor skills in a way that creates greater product value.

Production sharing is sometimes the only viable strategy available to companies to make products more competitive here and abroad. Under the U.S. production-sharing Harmonized Tariff Schedule provision 9802, U.S. materials that are assembled, processed or improved abroad can be shipped back to the U.S., incurring duty only on the foreign labor and non-U.S.-made materials. As such, these imports—which often contain substantial U.S. content—are often more price competitive than other imports with no U.S. content, and subject to lower Customs duties.

In the late 1980s, the U.S. International Trade Commission

conducted a survey of 900 U.S. firms engaged in production shar-ing. When asked what they would do if the production-sharing provision were eliminated, respondents indicated they would in-crease reliance on foreign-made parts or suffer a loss of U.S. market share to foreign competitors not using U.S.-made components. Their responses, ranked according to frequency, were:

- Turn to foreign suppliers of components.
- Discontinue producing labor-intensive products and import them from East Asia.
- Move all manufacturing to Asia.
- Cut back U.S. production and target a market niche not threat-ened by imports.
- Go out of business.

These options are poor alternatives to production sharing, es-pecially since the strategy is responsible for generating new jobs and retaining those that would be lost due to intense foreign com-petition, according to the U.S. International Trade Commission.

FAQ: Do other countries engage in production sharing?

Talking Points:

Yes, they do. The number of firms around the world engaging in cross-border manufacturing is on the rise. In fact, back in 1998, it involved more than $800 billion or at least 30 percent of total manufacturing trade annually, according to the World Bank report *Just How Big Is Global Production Sharing?* Today it is certainly much higher. And the growing interdependence of countries utilizing this strategy also is evident, since trade in components and parts has been growing considerably faster than trade in finished products.

Companies in Japan, Korea and Taiwan co-produce in China, Indonesia, Malaysia, Thailand and the Philippines primarily to reduce their labor costs. In the EU, most co-production involves apparel, auto parts and electronic products, and occurs mainly in Poland, the Czech Republic, Hungary and Slovenia—countries with inexpensive but well-educated labor forces. A growing share of EU co-production is taking place in Northern Africa.

As a result of its growing use, production sharing for many companies has become a necessary strategy used simply to keep up as opposed to achieving a competitive advantage. But while co-production has allowed many producers to cut costs, improve technology and increase their level of competitiveness, not all have benefited. Some companies have invested in foreign-based production sharing facilities only to find unexpectedly low levels of productivity, excessively high turnover, poor infrastructure and a corrupt legal system. Consequently, many of these firms have abandoned their efforts.

FAQ: How has worldwide sourcing changed?

Talking Points:

In the past, global sourcing typically involved the purchase of foreign goods. In recent years, however, worldwide sourcing, also referred to as offshoring or outsourcing abroad, has expanded to include services. (Note: unlike production sharing, which utilizes U.S. components and materials in the final product, products purchased overseas may or may not include U.S. components and materials.)

Labor-intensive services have begun to be outsourced in India, the Philippines, Malaysia and other countries with large, well-educated, English-speaking labor pools. This has been made possible by new technologies that allow for the transfer of huge amounts of information around the world at minimal costs—coupled with the ability to digitize and computerize many services.

Since global sourcing is structurally simpler in the service sector than in the manufacturing sector in terms of resources, space and equipment requirements, worldwide sourcing of services is expected to grow. However, the McKinsey Global Institute report says that fear of massive job losses is unfounded, since the vast majority of services cannot be purchased abroad and will remain in the U.S.

But the report goes much further. It estimates that two-thirds of the economic benefits from sourcing services in India flow back to the U.S. In turn, U.S. companies that outsource generate greater profits, become more globally competitive, and are better positioned to sell more goods and services worldwide. As stated earlier, the Bureau of Labor Statistics predicts that the number of U.S. jobs will increase by 21.3 million from 2002 to 2012. This figure accommodates the projected loss of jobs due to global outsourcing, manufacturing abroad or other reasons. Note: for more information on this concept, see Part II.

Very important is the issue of insourcing: the movement of foreign jobs to the United States or put another way, the expansion into the United States by foreign headquartered multinational firms. According to *Insourcing Jobs: Making the Global Economy Work for America*, by Professor Matthew J. Slaughter of the Dartmouth College Tuck School of Business, foreign companies operating in the United States employed 5.4 million Americans with a U.S. payroll of $307 billion in 2002.

Protectionism

FAQ: What are the costs of protectionism?

Talking Points:

Although in some instances protectionism may help fledgling industries for limited periods of time, current and decades-old studies indicate that protectionism actually has severe negative consequences. Reducing the number of imports through the use of trade barriers only raises the costs of goods and services to consumers and results in net job losses.

According to the 2002 U.S. International Trade Commission report, *The Economic Effects of Significant U.S. Import Restraints*, if all U.S. trade barriers had been simultaneously eliminated in 1999, 175,000 full-time workers would have been displaced, with the textile and apparel sector incurring nearly 90 percent of that loss. This would have represented only one one-hundredth of 1 percent of the 1999 labor force of 122.1 million. However, the report indicates, 192,400 full-time jobs would have been created, resulting in a net gain of nearly 17,400 jobs. In addition, total output would have increased by $58.8 billion.

The WTO determined in 1988 that $3 billion was added annually to grocery bills of U.S. consumers to support sugar import restrictions. In the late 1980s, U.S. trade barriers on textile and clothing imports raised the cost of these goods to consumers by 58 percent. And when the U.S. limited Japanese car imports in the early 1980s, car prices rose by 41 percent between 1981 and 1984. The objective was to save American jobs. However, in the end, more jobs were lost due to a reduction in the sale of U.S.-made automobiles, according to the WTO.

Additionally, the report *Trade, Jobs and Manufacturing* contends that if import barriers on sugar products were eliminated, imports would surge by almost 50 percent and domestic production would fall by 7.2 percent. The resulting job losses in sugar-related industries would total 2,290 out of 16,400 full-time industry jobs—a small number compared to an average of 235,000 net new jobs the U.S. economy created each month leading up to 1999, the year the report was released.

In December 2003, President George W. Bush announced his decision to remove the steel tariffs he had imposed 21 months earlier. Nevertheless, the damage was done. U.S. steel users incurred massive price increases as well as major supply disruptions, according to William Gaskin, president of the Precision Metaforming Association, as reported in a June 2004 CATO report. The higher prices caused many steel-consuming industries to shrink. In the end, more jobs were likely lost than gained.

Commenting on the costs of protectionism to consumers, Peter Sutherland, former Director General of General Agreement on Tariffs and Trade (GATT), now the World Trade Organization (WTO), said, "It is high time that governments made clear to consumers just how much they pay—in the shops and as taxpayers—for decisions to protect domestic industries from import competition. Virtually all protection means higher prices. And someone has to pay, either the consumer or, in the case of intermediate goods, another producer. The result is a drop in real income and an inability to buy other products and services."

FAQ: Does protectionism effectively save jobs in failing industries over the long term?

Talking Points:

No, it does not. Scholars and leaders of industry alike agree that even if a greater level of protectionism were implemented, low-technology jobs would still be replaced by technology or shifted to lower-wage locations over time. Robert Reich, former U.S. Secretary of Labor, stated that "Even if millions of workers in developing nations were not eager to do these [low-technology] jobs at a fraction of the wages of U.S. workers, such jobs would still be vanishing. Domestic competition would drive companies to cut costs by installing robots, computer integrated manufacturing systems or other means of replacing the work of unskilled Americans with machinery that can be programmed to do much the same thing."

There are many examples of technology raising worker productivity and business efficiency, where output increased or remained the same while utilizing fewer, higher-paid workers. According to *Trade, Jobs and Manufacturing,* a 1999 CATO study by Daniel Griswold, "In the last two decades, tens of thousands of telephone operators and bank tellers have been displaced from their jobs, not by imports, but by computerized switching and automated teller machines."

On this point, Sutherland says, "Maybe consumers would feel better about paying higher prices if they could be assured it was an effective way of maintaining employment. Unfortunately, the reality is that the cost of saving a job, in terms of higher prices and taxes, is frequently far higher than the wage paid to the workers concerned. In the end, in any case, the job often disappears as the protected companies either introduce new labor-saving technology or become less competitive. A far better approach would be to use the money to pay adjustment costs, like retraining programs and the provision of infrastructure."

In the early 19th century, the English Luddites attempted to destroy textile machines because they replaced weavers. Modern-day "Luddites" want to do essentially the same thing—but they have mistakenly attacked trade instead of technology. Explaining the impact of technology and its relationship with protectionism, Michael Licata, a senior economic development executive, tells the following story.

Each day, 10 fishermen ventured to the ocean to catch their family's food requirements. The task lasted all day. However, on one particular day, a fisherman brought a net he created by twining vines together. And in just six hours, he caught enough fish to supply all 10 families. Amazed, the other fishermen marveled over the new invention. One asked, "What are you going to do with all that fish? Your family can't eat all of them." "I guess you're right," said the net man. "I'll tell you what," said another, "I'll keep your roof from leaking if you give me enough fish to feed my family." Another said, "My wife has a garden, so I'll trade you vegetables for fish." And a third said, "I hate fishing. If you catch my fish from now on, I'll hunt game and gather your firewood in the forest." When the net man returned each day with his large catch of fish, he saw his wood chopped, vegetables near his door, and a brace of rabbits hanging on his fence. He even was able to sleep better since his roof no longer leaked during rainy nights. Others, too, benefited from various trades and ventured into other businesses. For example, one man learned to play an instrument he made out of wood and entertained villagers at night in exchange for goods and services. Another experimented with herbs and began curing certain illnesses. However, as specialization occurred and life improved for all 10 families, the fishing pole maker was not happy. His business worsened since fewer men now fished. Enraged, one night he sneaked over to the net man's hut and destroyed the invention. In the morning, the disaster was discovered and the day's allotment of fish went unmet. The next day all 10 original fishermen returned to their boats to fish. Leaky roofs went unfixed, firewood uncut, game uncaught, illnesses uncured and evening entertainment ceased. But, the fishing pole maker was happy at the expense of many.

FAQ: What is the protectionist worst case scenario?

Talking Points:

In the 1930s U.S. industrial production began to fall and U.S. farmers felt the effects of foreign agricultural competition. European agricultural recovery after World War I resulted in overproduction. As a result, international agricultural prices fell. The solution: on June 17, 1930, President Hoover signed the Smoot-Hawley Act that raised tariffs nearly 60 percent over their existing high rate of 44 percent. Although the act seemed like a good idea at the time, it effectively killed international trade. Within two years following the act's implementation, U.S. exports decreased by nearly two-thirds.

In anticipation of Smoot-Hawley's passage, France, Italy, India and Australia passed their own protectionist legislation. Others, such as Spain, Switzerland and Canada, followed suit. The result: export markets dried up and domestic industries slowed down. For the next eight years international trade declined. The unemployment rate in the United States rose to 25 percent in 1933. What began as a sincere attempt to aid U.S. industry made an international crisis of the highest order more severe.

Today, the potential negative impact of protectionism is no less severe. Larry Davidson, professor of Business Economics and Public Policy at the Indiana University Kelley School of Business finds that manufactured exports have been extremely important to economic vitality, manufacturing output and employment in 10 Northeast states analyzed in his recent report, *Exports of the Northeast Region 1996 to 2004*, prepared for the Council of State Governments Eastern Region. The report, co-authored by Benjamin Warolin and Lan Zhang, cites considerable strength in export growth from 1996 to 2004 of chemicals and pharmaceuticals to Germany and the Netherlands, and ever stronger gains of machinery sales to China and

Mexico. When it comes to identifying hot spots of export growth in 2004, the report identifies reliable partners like Japan, the United Kingdom, Germany and the Netherlands, as well as newcomers like China and South Korea. "Clearly, if the U.S. and its key industrial regions are to continue to benefit from export growth to Europe and Asia, they cannot hope to do this while at the same time protecting their industries from imports from these countries," said Davidson. As stated earlier, international trade has become an integral part of everyday life, accounting for 25 percent of U.S. economic growth in 2004. If the United States takes protectionist actions, our trading partners are sure to do the same.

FAQ: How do tariffs and non-tariff barriers operate?

Talking Points:

Tariff barriers—taxes or duties levied on imports of foreign products—originally were established to provide revenue for the federal government, predating income or property taxes. Today, however, they are viewed differently. In effect, tariffs increase the product price which discourages its demand and thereby insulates, to a degree, domestic producers from foreign competition. Each country places higher tariffs on goods determined to be import sensitive.

The most common form of duty or tariff is the ad valorem: a tax assessed on merchandise value. In addition, other types exist. Specific duties are those charged by weight, volume, length or any other unit (e.g., charging 10 cents per square yard on fabric). Compound duties call for both an ad valorem and a specific duty on the same product. Alternative duties are those in which the custom official calculates the ad valorem duty and the specific duty and applies whichever is higher. In addition to the above fees, an import processing fee, harbor tax, and other taxes, if further assessed, increase the exporter's costs.

Non-tariff barriers, on the other hand, are often hidden, and are not necessarily quantifiable or measurable. They typically include quotas, boycotts, licenses, health standards, local content requirements, restrictions on foreign investment, domestic government purchasing policies, exchange controls and subsidies, as well as formal and non-formal bureaucratic red tape. Like tariff barriers, non-tariff barriers often are used to inhibit the importation of products. In many sectors, environmental, labor and investment issues increasingly are being used in an abusive manner to discourage trade.

At times when it appears that foreign government subsidies for industry are decreasing, assistance by other means may be increasing.

Many analysts believe the Europeans, Japanese, and even the emerging markets are investing more and more of their resources to do battle with U.S. companies. In a sampling of about 200 overseas competitive projects tracked during an eight year period, it was estimated that U.S. firms lost approximately one-half of these due in part to government pressure—a hidden and non-quantifiable barrier to trade.

FAQ: How do global trade disputes, which often arise out of an attempt to protect an industry, affect U.S. companies and workers?

Talking Points:

The United States always has been a leading proponent of free trade. However, many now believe this leadership position is at stake—especially since U.S. willingness to accept WTO rulings is questioned. For example, both WTO and NAFTA committees have ruled that Canadian lumber subsidization evidence is insufficient. Nevertheless, the U.S. continues to impose tariffs on Canadian softwood lumber exports to the U.S. This dispute has been unresolved since 1982.

The U.S. is not alone in terms of non-compliance with international trade rulings. And, if the number of global trade disputes is any indication of unfair play, the U.S., EU and several other countries share company. Since 1995, the year the WTO was established, the international body has accepted about 30 trade dispute cases annually. As of April 6, 2005, the U.S. alone has been charged with 86 trade disputes; the EU or member states have been charged with 54, according to the Progressive Policy Institute.

In today's competitive world, national tax laws and subsidies have become extremely complex, resulting in numerous unintended consequences—including multiple trade disputes. For example, for decades, EU industries, such as aerospace and telecommunications, have been subsidized. This has boosted their international strength or shielded them from global competition. In addition, the EU has exempted its exporters from paying a value added tax, which, in effect, has reduced their tax burden.

Although Europe's tax loopholes and subsidies distort trade by artificially increasing the attractiveness of its exports, its indirect tax system is technically WTO-compliant. To counter this, the U.S. crafted the Foreign Sales Corporation (FSC) tax code in 1984. This was designed to help U.S. exporters compete more fairly with EU companies, as well as others around the world. Many U.S. companies claimed it was a success. In fact, a National Foreign Trade Council report stated that 3.5 million U.S. export-related jobs benefited from FSC tax incentives in 1999. However, the EU challenged the FSC rule through the WTO, and won in 2000. To appease the EU and global trade body, the U.S. repealed the law. In its place, the U.S. Congress created the Extraterritorial Income Exclusion (ETI) Act of 2000. But this law still didn't satisfy the EU. Consequently, the EU challenged it through the WTO and won.

To remedy the situation, on October 22, 2004, President George W. Bush signed legislation repealing ETI. The bill also reduced corporate tax rates for domestic manufacturers and simplified tax rules on overseas profits. Without this, it was argued prior to repealing ETI that approximately 6,000 U.S. exporters, who relied on ETI to compete, would have been hurt. Several years ago Boeing estimated that repealing ETI without a suitable replacement would result in the loss of nearly 10,000 of its high-tech jobs, as well as 23,000 more jobs with its suppliers. Why? In 2002, Boeing's heavily subsidized European rival, Airbus, was estimated to have received more than $30 billion in EU financial support. Boeing claimed this gave the EU conglomerate an unfair advantage. Furthermore, analysts believed this affected the entire U.S. aerospace industry that employed nearly 800,000 highly skilled workers in 2002. Nevertheless, for over a decade the Boeing-Airbus fight has continued to rage without a solution in sight. In fact, the heat was elevated in May 2005 when Airbus requested $1.7 billion subsidy in launch aid for its new A350 mid-range jetliner.

Should the number of trade disputes continue to climb resulting in retaliation, American exporters stand to suffer losses. Retaliatory actions, which typically come in the form of increased tariffs, raise the cost of American products in foreign markets. Often leading to decreased sales for U.S. companies, this can translate to fewer jobs for American workers. As a result, it is in the interest of the U.S., the EU and others to swiftly remedy disputes and focus on more profitable long-term trade relations.

Free Trade
FAQ: What are the theoretical benefits of free trade?

Talking Points:
International trade theory has its roots in the 18th-century writings of Adam Smith. Not only did he refute arguments for restricted trade, which relied on the belief that material gains acquired by one nation were done so at the expense of the other, but he demonstrated the potential gains of free trade. Thus, trade among nations is not a zero sum game, but rather, a win-win situation.

According to Smith, nations can increase their combined output if each specializes in producing the goods at which it is most efficient and then engages in trade with other nations. Each country will be better off, in terms of the quantity of goods available for consumption, resources expended and additional output obtained through specialization.

Demonstrated by David Ricardo, a prominent classical economist, even if a trading nation does not possess an absolute advantage in the production of a commodity, it will still gain by producing and exporting those products at which it has a comparative advantage. In other words, the less efficient nation should specialize in and export the commodity at which it has the least disadvantage. To understand this point, consider the following example on a personal level. If you can type letters faster than your assistant, who is paid considerably less than you are, should you put aside your more sophisticated and profitable projects so you can type? The answer is no. You are better off delegating the typing to your assistant even though you are more proficient at it.

Today the contemporary international trade environment is significantly different than what it was during the lives of Adam Smith and David Ricardo. Nevertheless, free trade principles remain valid. Michael Porter, a contemporary trade theorist, explains that the principal economic goal of a nation is to produce a high and rising standard of living for its citizens. Porter contends that the ability to do so depends on the productivity with which a nation's resources are employed. Productivity is defined as the value of the output produced by a unit of labor or capital. It depends on both quality and features of products as well as the efficiency in which they are produced. As such, the ability to export many goods produced with high productivity allows a nation to import many goods involving lower productivity. This is desirable because it translates into higher national productivity.

In pursuit of both increased productivity and international competitiveness, governments should promote trade without barriers— or free trade—without which the economic growth of a nation will be stunted. Overall, free trade promotes the creation of economies of scale, an increase in efficiency and competitiveness, a reduction of resources used in the production of goods and a higher standard of living. Yet, at the same time, governments also must provide safety nets for those who are unable to adapt.

Often unrecognized, the best example of totally free trade is the unobstructed trade among states in the United States. As a result, the United States is unquestionably the wealthiest single market and an extremely efficient producer of goods and services.

FAQ: Do small businesses benefit from free trade?

Talking Points:

Since 1992, trade agreements such as the Tokyo Round and the Uruguay Round of the GATT, the predecessor of the WTO, and NAFTA, as well as hundreds of other lesser-known trade agreements, have been negotiated and implemented by the United States. Without a doubt, small businesses have benefited from the resulting substantial reduction in foreign trade barriers.

Nevertheless, obstacles remain. For instance, some high foreign duties have prevented many small U.S. firms with limited resources from exporting. Large companies, however, often have circumvented these barriers by establishing a presence in the foreign country, achieving secure and competitive access. By the U.S. participating in trade agreements and thereby reducing and eliminating foreign tariffs, small companies' products can be more price competitive, enabling them to export more goods and create new jobs.

Foreign red tape or non-tariff barriers, such as import license requirements, also have prevented small companies from exporting. Again, large companies often have the resources to hire consultants or the in-house expertise to work through these sometimes hidden barriers. Small companies usually don't. By eliminating confusing red tape through trade agreements, small companies are put on a more level playing field and are better positioned to grow internationally. Additionally, small companies often are able to respond more quickly to market changes than large firms. This can give them an edge as the pace of global change quickens. Importantly, as more "niche" market opportunities present themselves—which may be considered insignificant in size for large multinationals—small firms often find them very profitable and well worth the pursuit.

FAQ: How is free trade different from a custom union or a common market?

Talking Points:

A free trade area is formed when two or more nations establish preferential trade liberalization policies by eliminating or substantially reducing trade barriers among themselves. A customs union surpasses free trade liberalization policies by establishing a common external tariff for non-members. A common market goes even further. Members eliminate restrictions on the movement of labor and capital among each other. Additionally, members may harmonize national policies to some degree, including monetary, fiscal and social policies, and concede a degree of political and legal control to a single ruling authority.

Most trade accords owe their success, at least in part, to prior reductions in trade barriers between the parties to the agreement. For example, the U.S.-Canada Free Trade Agreement was preceded in 1965 by the Automotive Products Trade Act (APTA), which allowed duty-free trade between the United States and Canada in almost all motor vehicles and parts. This resulted in extensive integration of motor vehicle production between the two countries.

Overall, free trade agreements, like custom unions and common markets, have had a major impact on trade and investment worldwide. In fact, they are responsible for shaping business relationships among companies across the globe. In order to succeed in the international environment, companies and organizations need to be aware of the impact trade agreements have had and will continue to have on their businesses and industries.

FAQ: How did trade liberalization policies give birth to the European Union?

Talking Points:

On April 18, 1951, the European Coal and Steel Community was formed. Its success prompted the March 25, 1957 signing of the Treaties of Rome, creating the European Economic Community (EEC) and the European Atomic Energy Community. On April 8, 1965, the three organizations merged into the European Communities, simply referred to as the European Community or EC. On July 8, 1968, the EC formally established a customs union. What prompted all this?

An economic decline in the 1970s, compounded by a recession in 1980, caused EC economies to stagnate. Declining confidence in EC policy and increased import competition from members and non-members alike resulted in individual EC countries establishing non-tariff barriers directed toward competitors, including other EC members. Consequently, industries became increasingly inefficient and less competitive with the United States, Japan and the newly industrialized countries of the Far East.

In an attempt to reverse this trend, in 1982, the European Council, composed of EC member nation heads, agreed that the completion of a unified market was a priority and requested that the EC Commission propose a timetable for removing all obstacles. In June 1985, the Commission released its white paper detailing a timetable ending December 31, 1992, for the implementation of some 300 directives or measures intended to eliminate all physical, technical and fiscal barriers to intra-EC trade. Essential to its success was the enactment of the 1987 Single European Act that changed EC voting procedure. This body has matured into a common market, now known as the European Union or EU. Policies include the elimination of barriers to labor and capital movements, coordinated monetary and fiscal policies, a common agricultural policy, use of common investment funds, and similar rules for wage and welfare payments.

International Organizations

FAQ: How have the World Trade Organization and its predecessor, the General Agreement on Tariffs and Trade, impacted trade?

Talking Points:

The General Agreement on Tariffs and Trade (GATT), established in 1947 in Geneva, Switzerland, was responsible for governing approximately 90 percent of world trade. It sought to liberalize trade and thereby improve the world trading system through a code of rules and a forum at which negotiations and other trade discussions took place. Importantly, it played a major role in the settlement of trade disagreements among member countries. The founders of GATT believed that increased international trade would promote an economic interdependence between countries, making wars between trading partners unthinkable.

GATT was responsible for reducing the international tariff average from 40 percent in 1947 to 5 percent in 1990. These reductions permitted international trade to expand tremendously, national incomes to increase substantially, and international competition to flourish, resulting in higher quality, lower priced goods. The organization was very successful at reducing international trade barriers. However, many analysts argued that it was not very successful at remedying less apparent forms of protection, such as non-tariff barriers. New protectionist tools, such as abusive uses of dumping legislation, labor and other issues, were recognized as the new non-tariff barriers. It was widely held that GATT would not be able to contain this.

In the early 1990s, GATT's inability to eliminate non-tariff barriers put the organization in jeopardy. Its incapacity to successfully remedy the U.S.-European Community disagreement over agricultural subsidies created doubt as to the organization's ability to meet future challenges. Furthermore, the decreasing level of world confidence in GATT contributed to the speed at which countries formed trading blocs. Since the successful conclusion of the GATT Uruguay Round Agreements, the degree of confidence in its successor organization, the World Trade organization(WTO), has risen significantly.

Established on January 1, 1995, the WTO deals with agriculture, textiles and clothing, banking, telecommunications, government purchases, industrial standards and product safety, food sanitation regulations, intellectual property and much more. By June 2005, the number of WTO members had reached 148 (in 1948 the GATT had 23 contracting parties). The WTO is a democratic organization whose agreements are adopted by consensus. Consequently, each country decides according to its legislative process whether or not it will be bound by WTO agreements.

FAQ: How did the Multifiber Arrangement emerge and what is its impact on textile and apparel?

Talking Points:

During the 1960s and 1970s, worldwide growth in the number of textile and apparel producers led to production overcapacity. As a result, the global supply of textiles and apparel exceeded the growth in demand. Competition intensified. As producers in developed countries attempted to protect their markets from imports originating in low-wage countries, bilateral trade policies emerged under an international framework.

The Arrangement Regarding International Trade in Textiles, more commonly known as the Multifiber Arrangement (MFA), was finalized at the end of 1973 and enacted in January 1974. Approximately 50 countries signed the original agreement, which was established and managed under the auspices of the General Agreement on Tariffs and Trade, the predecessor to the WTO. The MFA was considered general and became an umbrella arrangement under which bilateral agreements could be conducted, typically involving the implementation of import quotas. These agreements and quotas were necessary because importing countries, primarily developed countries, believed specific textile and apparel products imported from developing countries were disrupting their markets. As part of the new arrangement, provisions were included that monitored the implementation of the MFA, defined strict rules for determining market disruption, and permitted quotas to grow by 6 percent annually.

The original MFA was renegotiated in 1977 (MFA II, 1977-81). Although the United States was the leader in pursuing the original multilateral agreement, the European Community took the lead this time and pressed for an increasingly restrictive MFA. The 6-percent annual growth rate for quotas permitted in the first MFA was of particular concern to European Community (EC) representatives. Manufacturers argued that it was unfair for imports to increase by 6 percent a year when their own share of the domestic market was increasing at rates as slow as 1 percent. As a result, industry leaders sought to have the import growth rate tied to the domestic rate. Under the new Multifiber Arrangement, a less severe clause was added that allowed the EC to reduce certain quota growth rates below 6 percent.

The 1981 negotiations for renewal of the MFA (MFA III, 1981-86) were particularly difficult. From the perspective of both the EC and U.S. textile and apparel industries, MFA II—despite its increasingly restrictive features—was not effective in slowing the tide of imports. Developing countries became increasingly organized in pressing for their interests, however, and in the end they succeeded in implementing a less-restrictive "anti-surge" provision, which provided for special restraints in the event of "sharp and substantial increases" in imports of the most sensitive products. MFA III also tightened the definition of market disruption by requiring proof of a decline in the growth rate of per capita consumption.

U.S. officials went into the 1986 MFA renewal negotiations under heavy pressure from the domestic textile industry to provide increased protection from low-wage imports. During this period, EC industries were affected less by imports, enjoying a relatively healthy economic period. The EC, however, joined the United States and Canada in presenting a joint statement for the 1986 renewal (MFA IV, 1986-91). Although exporting countries were even more organized than in the past, their diverse composition continued to prevent full unity. In addition, they still lacked the bargaining power sufficient to counter the strength of the developed countries. Because quotas were based on past performance, smaller suppliers, usually from the least developed countries, had little opportunity to obtain substantial quota increases. In an effort to improve the exporting nations' bargaining position, the International Textiles and Clothing Bureau (ITCB) was established to represent their interests more effectively.

Throughout the GATT negotiations, textile and apparel trade provoked one controversy after another. By December 1988, ministers from 19 developing countries asserted their unwillingness to continue in the broader talks unless problems related to the Multifiber Arrangement were addressed. They requested a clear timetable for phaseout of the MFA. Representatives from developed countries found it hard to agree to the demands. As the GATT talks dragged on, various countries offered proposals for bringing textile trade back under mainstream GATT regulations. In 1990, U.S. officials offered a plan that provided quota allocations for each country which would be eliminated gradually, and an overall global quota, but the U.S. proposal encountered strong opposition from exporting nations. U.S. retailers and importers also believed the plan would be detrimental to their interests.

After GATT talks resumed in Brussels in December 1990, the new Agreements on Textiles and Clothing, which became known as the Brussels Draft, called for textile products to be integrated into GATT, eliminating quota restrictions in three stages. A year later, however, textile negotiations reached an impasse over certain issues related to phasing out the MFA. In December 1993, the Uruguay Round talks resumed, and after seven years of bitter deliberation, a GATT accord was finalized. The MFA was officially replaced by the Uruguay Round's final Agreements on Textiles and Clothing, which was enacted on January 1, 1995 as part of the WTO, the successor to GATT. Despite heavy developed country opposition to a 10-year phaseout of quotas, the agreement provided for the elimination of quotas on textiles and apparel over the decade ending January 1, 2005. After this date, only tariffs should remain.

As a result of the abolished quotas, prices are anticipated to fall and major Western buyers are expected to narrow their sources to large vertically integrated Asian suppliers. China, in particular, is expected to gain an increasingly large share of textile and clothing production.

As stated earlier, the WTO estimates that the U.S. quota on Chinese imports of apparel had the equivalent effect of a 34 percent tax on Chinese imports. By eliminating this tax, absent offsetting trade barriers or currency changes, China's share of U.S. imports is projected to rise from 16 percent to 50 percent; its share of the U.S. apparel market is estimated to rise from 5.4 percent to 22.5 percent. Much of this will be at the expense of past suppliers, including Bangladesh and the Philippines.

Currency Issues

FAQ: How does the value of the dollar impact the U.S. economy?

Talking Points:

The effects of a rising or declining dollar are complex and not always well understood. When the dollar decreases in value, U.S. exports typically become more attractive abroad. In turn, companies selling more goods and services often hire more workers. But a decreasing dollar has other consequences. For example, U.S. manufacturers who rely on imported components and materials find it more costly to produce their goods. In turn, these manufacturers may absorb this added cost, which will reduce corporate profits and possibly impact hiring. Or, they may pass this increase on to consumers, which could lead to inflation. Additionally, a dollar that is weakening or declining in value for lengthy periods of time or at a rapid pace can dampen investor confidence and result in less U.S. inbound investment. In turn, this can make it difficult to finance budget deficits and may lead to higher interest rates. Thus, business expansion becomes more costly and compromises the ability of companies to hire new employees.

A rising dollar, which often leads to increased foreign investment in the United States, makes U.S. exports of goods and services more expensive abroad and can result in lost export deals. Additionally, according to Fred Bergsten of the Institute for International Economics, every 1 percent rise in the U.S. dollar's trade-weighted value boosts the U.S. current account deficit by at least $10 billion. If perceived as unsustainable, a rising current account deficit can negatively affect confidence in the U.S. economy, and in turn, accelerate downward pressure on the dollar.

Overall, a rising or declining dollar has a number of positive and negative consequences. But one thing is certain: a stable and predictable dollar is extremely important to the well being of the United States. (For information on the Chinese currency, see Part I).

FAQ: How has the value of the dollar fluctuated since the 1970s?

Talking Points:

In March 1973, the Federal Reserve's Nominal Major Currencies Dollar Index was set at 100. In March 1985, the U.S. dollar reached its highest level at 143.90. About 10 years later, in April 1995, it fell to 80.33. Within seven years it climbed up to its recent peak of 111.98 in February 2002, as compared to major currencies.

Why did the dollar rise through February 2002? During the 1990s, foreign investment flowed into the United States at an unprecedented pace. The longest U.S. peacetime expansion on record, strong productivity gains and a stock market with exceptional returns attracted capital from all corners of the globe. Additionally, after the Asian crisis and uncertainty over the value of the euro, investment looking for a safe haven poured into the U.S.

Why did the dollar lose value after February 2002? By early 2002, the U.S. current account deficit, the budget deficit, less foreign investment in the U.S., a volatile American stock market and a decline in U.S. consumer confidence all contributed to the dollar's subsequent decline. As a result, the dollar fell to an all time low of 80.11 in December 2004. As of July 2005, the dollar stood at 85.77.

Value of the U.S. Dollar
Federal Reserve's Nominal Major Currencies Index
January 1973 - July 2005

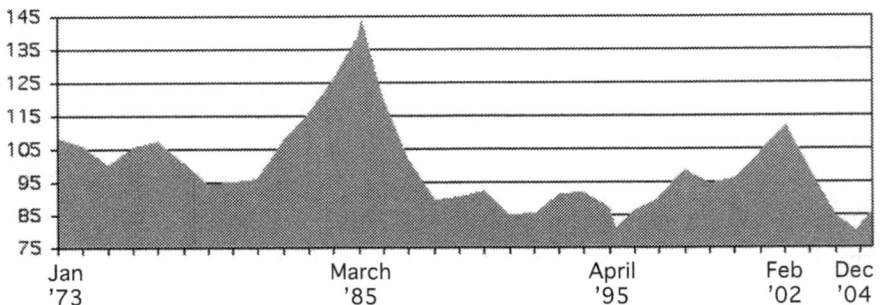

Source: U.S. Federal Reserve

FAQ: Has the weaker dollar slowed U.S. imports?

Talking Points:

As the dollar decreased, many assumed that U.S. imports would slow since it would require more U.S. dollars to buy foreign goods. But as of June 2, 2005, this has not materialized. According to Catherine Mann of the Institute for International Economics, "With the exception of oil, imports have not become more expensive. One reason is that about 30 percent of our imports come from countries whose currencies have either moved little (the Thai baht), stayed stable (the Chinese yuan), or fallen (the Mexican peso) against the dollar.

But another reason is the worldwide decline during the 1990s of what some economists call 'pass-through rates,' that is, the extent to which changes in the exchange rate induce changes in a country's import and export prices. A study by economists Linda Goldberg and Jose Manuel Campa found that pass-through rates for the United States were significantly less than for other industrial countries. A 10 percent change in the dollar has generally yielded only a 2.5 percent change in American import prices within one quarter, and only a 4 percent price change after several quarters. Another study by the Federal Reserve found that the pass-through was nearly zero." Mann notes several factors explain a low pass-through rate, including low global inflation and the fact that foreign exporters are willing to take smaller margins in order to retain U.S. marketshare. As a result, Mann says it will take a bigger drop in the dollar to change import prices enough to slow the American appetite for foreign goods.

FAQ: What is the impact of the euro?

Talking Points:

Unlike the original 15 EU members—Austria, Belgium, Denmark, Finland, France, Germany, Greece, Ireland, Italy, Luxembourg, the Netherlands, Portugal, Spain, Sweden and the United Kingdom— the 10 new EU accession nations must adopt the euro when they fulfill specific requirements. This may take several years. But given their limited circulation and high levels of currency volatility, joining the euro area, also known as Euroland or the Eurozone, is an advantage in terms of stability and confidence.

Three of the original 15 EU members have a very different set of concerns and issues regarding the Eurozone. In past nationwide referendums, both Denmark and Sweden voted against euro participation. And according to analysts, the United Kingdom is unlikely to adopt it any time soon. Nationalists from these countries argue that euro participation will erode national sovereignty and hand over power to the European Central Bank whose "one size fits all" policies may not be welcomed. Furthermore, many are concerned that the single currency could lead to a political union that may promote legislation they do not support. The UK, which has been especially critical of the euro, has established five economic tests it says must be met before it calls a referendum. Prime Minister Tony Blair supports adopting the euro. But the Tories, the opposing conservative party, are against this in the immediate future. Britain's attachment to its relatively stable pound sterling, which has an unbroken history of more than 900 years and has dominated global trade for decades, is proving difficult to break.

The Eurozone, which currently represents a population of 305 million people, has benefited from the single European currency in a number of ways. According to an EU study, the establishment of the euro eliminated transaction costs estimated at 0.5 percent of GDP.

Other studies estimated this cost closer to 1 percent. An International Monetary Fund study projects the euro will increase GDP growth in participating member economies each year, and by almost 3 percent in 2010. Plus, greater macroeconomic stability and reduced governmental deficits are anticipated in an economically stronger Euroland. These and other benefits generated by the euro are attractive to newcomers.

It is estimated that approximately 60 percent of world trade is denominated in U.S. dollars. This may change. As new EU members adopt the euro, they will request their U.S. partners to transact business in the currency. And, as the EU and Euroland expand (Bulgaria and Romania may join the EU by 2007), complying with this request likely will give U.S. companies a competitive advantage over companies that don't.

FAQ: How did the Mexican peso crisis affect the United States?

Talking Points:

Currency instability in developing countries negatively impacts U.S. exporters and investors, and harms our economy's ability to create jobs. For example, on December 20, 1994, on the verge of entering the second year of NAFTA, the economic situation drastically changed. An attempted currency adjustment by the Mexican government accelerated out of control. The Mexican government expanded its exchange rate band by 15 percent in an attempt to allow the peso to adjust downward. Within two days pressures mounted and currency reserves used to prop up the peso quickly dwindled. As a result, the peso was allowed to float freely. Shortly thereafter, it nose-dived.

From December 20, 1994 to March 1995, the peso dropped about 40 percent in value as compared to the U.S. dollar. Like falling dominoes, what began as a short-term liquidity crisis, turned into a full panic. The Mexican stock market dropped precipitously. Most investors whose money came due did not reinvest in the country. As the value of the peso declined, the Mexican government was forced to raise short term interest rates by a dramatic amount to prevent a massive outflow of capital invested in Mexico and to fight inflation. At the time, a significant percentage of Mexican debt was in the form of tesobonos, securities denominated in dollars but paid in pesos. Tesobonos were designed to attract foreign capital by shielding foreign investors from exchange rate risk. Approximately $774 million worth of tesobonos matured on December 28, 1994; another $5.2 billion came due mid-February 1995. A total of approximately $28 billion in dollar denominated debt came due in the first half of 1995—an amount which had to be paid out in order to maintain some semblance of stability.

This situation, coupled with the assassination of Luis Donaldo

Colosio, the Institutional Revolutionary Party (PRI) presidential candidate and former Secretary for Urban Development and Ecology, raised questions among foreign investors as to Mexico's political stability. The assassination of Francisco Ruiz Massleu, a senior ranking PRI official, added to this uncertainty. These events, combined with unrest in the southern state of Chiapas, further fueled investor skepticism. Mexican fallout quickly spread to Brazil and Argentina, whose stock markets fell, along with those in other developing countries worldwide. Investors received what some have referred to as a "wake-up call," reminding them that political and economic instability can largely affect growth prospects in developing countries. In turn, U.S. exporters and investors must remember they too can be subject to considerable economic difficulties.

FAQ: How did the Asian financial crisis impact the United States?

Talking Points:

During the 1990s, Southeast Asian countries increasingly pegged their currencies to the U.S. dollar. After mid-1995, the U.S. dollar began to appreciate. As this occurred, Southeast Asian exports became more expensive while pressure mounted on their national exchange rates. In late 1996, foreign investors questioned Thailand's ability to repay its loans and began to move their money out of the country. Fearing a loss in the Thai baht's value, foreign investors and Thai companies began in February 1997 to convert the currency into U.S. dollars—accelerating a devaluation. With diminished reserves, the Thai central bank was forced to let the baht float downward.

Fearing neighboring countries shared many of the same weaknesses as Thailand, confidence in Malaysia, Indonesia and South Korea plummeted, resulting in a regional financial crisis. Consequently, economic growth in emerging Asian countries, excluding China, dropped precipitously.

Regions of the U.S. that were more dependent on exports to East Asia were affected to a greater extent than less dependent regions. Western states, such as Washington, Oregon, Arizona, California and Alaska, were more affected due to their higher concentration of exports to East Asia which included aircraft, semiconductors, electrical equipment and processed foods. Parts of the farm belt, the industrial Midwest and southern states were affected to a lesser degree. The Northeast, including New York, New Jersey, Pennsylvania and Connecticut, probably were impacted the least since a smaller percentage of their exports targeted the affected region. Additionally, many U.S. companies that were invested in the most affected Asian countries experienced severe difficulties.

NAFTA
FAQ: What is the impact of NAFTA on the United States?

Talking Points:

Formal NAFTA negotiations began in June 1991 and were completed in August 1992. The trade accord, ratified by both the U.S. House of Representatives and the Senate in November 1993, was implemented on January 1, 1994. Although more than a decade has passed, the question of whether NAFTA has had a positive or negative impact still persists. The perceived loss of U.S. economic preeminence vis-à-vis the rest of the world, coupled with the reduction in the number of U.S. manufacturing jobs, have generated frustration among many Americans. In addition, in this period of globalization, the fear of losing one's job is echoed daily. Without foundation, much of this frustration has been vented on NAFTA.

NAFTA is the most misunderstood trade agreement in memory. Due to a massive dissemination of misinformation by anti-NAFTA interests, including Ross Perot in the early 1990s, a large segment of the U.S. population continues to believe that NAFTA is not in the interest of the United States and will accelerate the loss of U.S. jobs and a decline in U.S. wages. Ironically, through NAFTA, the exact opposite has occurred.

Although it is easy to identify a lost job, it is difficult to identify a job gained as a result of trade with a specific country or region. Nevertheless, there's no doubt that NAFTA has generated a net increase in jobs in the United States. According to *NAFTA At Five Years*, published by the Council of the Americas and The U.S. Council of the Mexico-U.S. Business Committee, "NAFTA has led to more high-quality, better-paying jobs for U.S. workers." Between January 1994 and October 1998, the report states that the U.S. economy created 14.2 million jobs, "and many of these jobs can reasonably be attributed to NAFTA."

Based on job estimation formulas provided by the United States Trade Representative, NAFTA resulted in a net gain of over 900,000 jobs in the United States from 1994 through December 31, 1999. This figure accounts for the loss of jobs attributed to NAFTA by the NAFTA-Transitional Adjustment Assistance program (NAFTA-TAA) during this period. In 2000, Raul Hinojosa-Ojeda and others put the job net gain number closer to 74,000 annually. Regardless of the exact number, it is clear that NAFTA has provided a net gain in jobs.

But job gains are only one indicator of benefit. According to *The U.S. Employment Impact of North American Integration After NAFTA: A Partial Equilibrium Approach*, published by the North American Integration and Development Center at UCLA, "In general, job gain/loss accounting methodologies should not be used to evaluate the relative benefits of trade... What is much more significant as a measure of trade policy is the impact on economies of scale, technological change, new investments and productivity growth in the liberated sectors and the ability of the economy as a whole to reap benefits from these productivity increases."

Stated in *NAFTA At Five Years*, "NAFTA has fostered growth in cross-border investment that has improved the competitiveness of American companies, and consequently, their ability to keep high-skill, high-wage jobs in the United States. Hence, NAFTA's positive impact on the quality of jobs has been significant, while its overall impact on the number of U.S. jobs has been positive as well."

The increase in U.S.-Mexican trade since the implementation of NAFTA is a very positive factor. In fact, Mexico has become the United States' second largest export market. Mexico also has helped North America compete with an increasingly growing EU. But as stated earlier, increased trade in goods and services only represents a portion of NAFTA's benefits. Since U.S. gross domestic product was 20 times larger than Mexico's prior to the implementation of the agreement, and U.S. tariffs on Mexican goods already averaged a low 2 percent, the free trade agreement would not have a significant impact on the U.S. economy. "NAFTA was more about foreign policy than about the domestic economy," says Dan Griswold, director of the Center for Trade Policy Studies at the Washington, DC-based CATO Institute. "Its biggest payoff for the United States has been to institutionalize our southern neighbor's turn away from centralized protectionism and toward decentralized, democratic capitalism. By that measure, NAFTA has been a spectacular success."

Importantly, the typical Mexican boom-and-bust-cycle, high inflation, large debt, and the election-cycle economic crises seem to be things of the past. This has resulted in a more stable environment, increasing Mexico's level of global attractiveness in terms of its ability to capture foreign direct investment.

The Congressional decision to ratify NAFTA did not simply concern a trade agreement among the United States, Canada and Mexico. Rather, it was a decision on the direction of the United States, defining our perceived strengths and weaknesses, our level of confidence and courage, and a determination on how we, as a nation, would conduct ourselves in the new post-Cold War era. The world was closely watching the NAFTA vote. Ratification of NAFTA signaled that the United States was ready for the challenges of the 21st century. A "no" vote, however, would have been perceived as a retreat by the United States into policies of isolationism and protectionism. European and East Asian nations would have been more likely to turn inward. Most importantly, well-paying American jobs would have been lost. According to Federal Reserve Chairman Alan Greenspan, rejection of NAFTA would have had "a very wrenching effect" on the United States and the entire region.

FAQ: What were the original objectives and hopes of each NAFTA party?

Talking Points:

Both Canada and Mexico initiated NAFTA with the United States for a variety of reasons. In January 1990, Mexican President Carlos Salinas de Gortari visited Europe to promote foreign investment that would support the Mexican trade liberalization process. He found the Europeans preoccupied with Eastern Europe. It became apparent that Europe would not be a sufficient source of investment and exports. Mexico would have to depend upon U.S. investment and markets to increase productivity, exports and wages. Through a U.S.-Mexico free trade agreement, President Salinas hoped to stimulate Mexican economic growth through increased trade and investment. President Salinas also saw that a free trade agreement would likely prevent future Mexican presidents from deviating from his economic policies which he believed were essential to provide the stability necessary to promote long-term economic growth.

From Mexico's perspective, the anticipated benefits of greater economic integration included increased and secure access to U.S. and Canadian markets; achievement of international credibility and a gain of foreign investment; improved domestic confidence in Mexico's economic future and the return of flight capital; access to U.S. and Canadian technology and expertise; the development of economies of scale; higher productivity; a movement toward greater specialization; an increase in jobs and wages resulting in a higher standard of living with a more equal income distribution; improvement of working conditions; and a reduction in the so called brain drain or loss of educated workers through migration.

From Canada's perspective, the expected benefits of NAFTA included better access to Mexico's large and growing market; establishment of guarantees protecting intellectual property rights;

enhanced competitiveness at home and abroad; establishment of long-term guarantees protecting Canadian direct foreign investment; the development of economies of scale; greater productivity; a movement toward greater specialization; and availability of less-expensive products. (Note: NAFTA incorporated the benefits Canada already had derived from the U.S.-Canada Free Trade Agreement.)

President George H. Bush and Mexican President Salinas defined a U.S.-Mexican free trade agreement as a process of gradual and comprehensive elimination of trade barriers between the United States and Mexico, including the full, phased elimination of import tariffs; the elimination or fullest possible reduction of non-tariff trade barriers, such as import quotas, licenses and technical barriers to trade; the establishment of clear, binding protection for intellectual property rights; fair and expeditious dispute settlement procedures; and other means to improve and expand the flow of goods, services and investment between the United States and Mexico.

The United States had several fundamental objectives in pursuing a free trade agreement with Canada and Mexico. These included increasing U.S. exports to Mexico, thereby growing the number of well-paying U.S. jobs; the continued pursuit of Mexican trade and investment reforms, especially intellectual property rights, which would generate substantial new opportunities for U.S. firms; more efficient uses of natural and human resources in North America, in turn promoting U.S. world competitiveness; and Mexican economic growth and prosperity, increasing the Mexican standard of living and reducing the number of undocumented Mexican immigrants in the United States.

On February 5, 1991, the United States, Canada and Mexico issued a joint communiqué formally proposing a North American pact, they said, "would link our three economies in bold and different ways."

FAQ: How did NAFTA provide for the elimination of Mexican tariffs on U.S. goods?

Talking Points:

Duties on goods identified in "category A," which had the fastest tariff phase-out rate, were eliminated entirely on January 1, 1994. According to the U.S. International Trade Commission, this represented 31 percent of U.S. goods exported to Mexico (based on goods traded in 1990). Duties on goods in category B were removed in five equal annual stages beginning on January 1, 1994. This represented 17.4 percent of goods exported to Mexico. Duties on goods in category C were removed in 10 equal annual stages—representing 31.8 percent. Duties on goods in category C+ were to be removed in 15 equal annual stages—representing 1.4% of U.S. goods exported to the United States. And duties on goods in category D would continue to be duty free. This represented 17.9 percent of U.S. exports to Mexico.

Without NAFTA, Mexico would have had the right under international law to raise most of its duties to 50 percent. Under NAFTA, Mexico has been prevented from raising its duties above specific rates. Importantly, the United States, Mexico and Canada agreed on several occasions to accelerate the tariff reduction stages.

FAQ: How do NAFTA rules of origin operate?

Talking Points:

In an attempt to confine NAFTA benefits to North America, rules of origin were devised such that, when applied to a particular product, define the product's origin. As a result, only products that originate in North America are accorded free trade status—entering the United States, Mexico or Canada duty-free.

Concerns that non-North American companies would use Mexico as an export platform were addressed in NAFTA. For example, if two Japanese components are shipped to Mexico, undergo "simple assembly" there, and then are exported to the United States, under the NAFTA rules of origin, the finished product would not be classified as a Mexican product. Rather, it would be classified as a Japanese product. As a result, U.S. Customs would assess the same duty as if the product were shipped directly from Japan to the United States.

Under these origin requirements, products wholly obtained in North America, such as minerals extracted from the ground, undeniably satisfy these rules. However, products that embody overseas parts or materials must be substantially transformed in North America in order to satisfy the transformation requirements stipulated in NAFTA. For example, live chickens imported from Europe into the United States enter under a particular U.S. harmonized code. If processed in the United States into chicken cutlets, the product then takes on an entirely different tariff code classification. Thus, the cutlets would have been sufficiently transformed to be considered a U.S. product. If exported to Mexico, the cutlets would then qualify for duty-free treatment.

In some cases, a product must satisfy both transformation and content requirements. For example, hair dryer parts imported into Mexico from Japan and South Korea will arrive under parts classifications. When assembled with North American parts, the sum of the parts becomes a hand-held hair dryer. At this point, tariff transformation rules have been satisfied, but percentage content requirements also must be met.

New Trade Agreements
FAQ: What is the impact of the U.S.-Chilean Free Trade Agreement?

Talking Points:

On September 3, 2003, after years of intense negotiations, President George W. Bush signed the U.S.-Chile and U.S.-Singapore Free Trade Agreements. As a result, Chile and Singapore joined Israel, Canada, Mexico, and Jordan to become the United States' fifth and sixth free trade partners.

As the first comprehensive trade agreement between the United States and a South American country, the U.S.-Chile Free Trade Agreement is anticipated to boost bilateral trade and investment. Largely modeled after NAFTA, the Chilean accord encourages progress on the Free Trade Agreement of the Americas, which is anticipated to be completed in the near future.

Chile, the most free trade-oriented economy in South America, has negotiated several free trade agreements without U.S. involvement. In 1997 alone, Chile implemented a free trade agreement with Mercosur (the Southern Cone Common Market which includes Argentina, Brazil, Paraguay, and Uruguay), Mexico and Canada. And the EU became Chile's largest supplier of goods in 2001, primarily due to the EU-Chile 1996 Framework Agreement, which covers political, trade and economic cooperation. The EU-Chile Association Agreement, concluded in April 2002, is projected to enhance the EU-Chile relationship even more.

In the past, the absence of a U.S.-Chile free trade agreement put U.S. companies at a competitive disadvantage. For example, in October 2001 the National Association of Manufacturers released a study on losses in American exports to Chile since 1997, the year Chile established a free trade agreement with Canada. The report indicated that U.S. companies lost $800 million a year—that's more than $2 million a day—as a result of not being involved in that agreement. Until the U.S.-Chile accord was implemented, Canadian goods entered Chile duty-free, putting U.S. goods at a competitive disadvantage.

Until 1997, U.S. products were highly competitive in Chile and captured a growing share of Chile's import market. However, after 1997, the U.S. share of Chile's import market suddenly began to decline. In fact, according to the National Association of Manufacturers, it dropped from 24 percent to approximately 18 percent. This loss did not occur in other Latin American markets. In many ways, the U.S.-Chile trade agreement will level the playing field.

In the words of former U.S. Trade Representative Robert Zoellick, the U.S.-Chile accord "not only slashes tariffs, it reduces barriers to services, protects leading-edge intellectual property, keeps pace with new technologies, ensures regulatory transparency and provides effective labor and environmental enforcement." Upon implementation of the U.S.-Chile Free Trade Agreement, more than 85 percent of bilateral trade in consumer and industrial products became tariff free. This includes agricultural and construction equipment, autos and parts, computers and other information technology, medical equipment and paper products, according to the USTR. Additionally, more than three-quarters of U.S. farm goods will enter Chile duty free within four years, while all remaining tariffs will be phased out within 12 years.

Under the free trade agreement, greater access is expected for U.S. professionals, banks and insurance, telecommunications, securities and express delivery companies. Greater protection will be accorded to U.S. digital products, such as software, music, text and videos. Plus, protection of U.S. patents and trade secrets will surpass all previous agreements. Overall, the deal will establish a secure and more predictable legal framework for U.S. investors operating in Chile, according to USTR.

Chile is one of Latin America's most dynamic markets. Although its population is only 15 million and its economy is roughly 1.5 percent the size of the U.S. economy, Chile is considered one of the region's most promising markets. A study published by the University of Michigan and Tufts University estimates that the U.S.-Chile trade agreement will expand U.S. GDP by $4.2 billion and Chilean GDP by $700 million annually.

FAQ: What is the expectation of the Dominican Republic-Central American Free Trade Agreement?

Talking Points:

The primary goal of the Dominican Republic-Central American Free Trade Agreement (DR-CAFTA) is to eliminate barriers to trade in goods, agriculture, services and investment between the United States and the Dominican Republic, Costa Rica, El Salvador, Guatemala, Honduras and Nicaragua. DR-CAFTA is anticipated to give U.S. exporters and investors greater access to Central American markets, strengthen North-South ties, promote the rule of law in the region and foster economic growth there by granting the DR-CAFTA countries preferential access to U.S. markets.

In January 2003, when DR-CAFTA negotiations began, it was estimated that an agreement would be reached by December 2003, with a vote in Congress soon afterward. This did not occur. Sticking points involving agriculture (especially sugar), textiles, telecommunications, insurance and intellectual property protection proved difficult to remedy. Nevertheless, negotiations were completed. Greater difficulties, however, occurred in Washington, D.C.

On June 30, 2005, the Senate passed DR-CAFTA by a vote of 54 to 45. And after final deal making, the House vote came to an end a few minutes after midnight on July 28, 2005. The result: 217 to 215 in favor of passage.

As repeated throughout this book, free trade issues are receiving a great deal of negative attention in Washington and in many Congressional districts. The most controversial issues stem from the loss of U.S. manufacturing jobs. In the end, CAFTA became a lightning rod for those unhappy with U.S. economic conditions. This has, to some extent, overshadowed the advantages DR-CAFTA brings.

For example, more than 20 Central American trade agreements—

without U.S. involvement—have granted preferences to products from Mexico, Canada, Chile and several other nations. This has put U.S. exporters at a competitive disadvantage. U.S. apple growers, for instance, shipped nearly $4 million worth of apples to Costa Rica in 2002. To the disadvantage of these U.S. exporters, Costa Rica applied a 15 percent import tariff, while Canadian apples imported by Costa Rica entered duty free.

Prior to the implementation of the DR-CAFTA accord, the U.S. weighted average tariff rate on DR-CAFTA countries was 2.6 percent, according to the World Bank. This reflected the fact that approximately 80 percent of DR-CAFTA imports already entered the United States duty free. On the other hand, the weighted average tariff rate on U.S. goods was 10.1. percent in the Dominican Republic, 5.8 percent in Costa Rica, 6.1 percent in El Salvador, 5.8 percent in Guatemala, 7.3 percent in Honduras, and 2.3 percent in Nicaragua, the World Bank says. Under the agreement, DR-CAFTA countries will immediately eliminate 80 percent of their tariffs on U.S. goods and the remainder will be phased out over 10 years, according to the U.S. Trade Representative.

By reducing tariffs on U.S. goods and services, DR-CAFTA will level the playing field for U.S. firms and accelerate U.S. exports to the region. In addition, many U.S. textile producers believe the accord will boost DR-CAFTA apparel output. Why? DR-CAFTA countries typically utilize U.S.-produced cotton and textiles; Asian apparel producers generally do not. Plus, many U.S. policymakers hope the accord will act as a stepping stone to the creation of the Free Trade Area of the Americas.

The DR-CAFTA countries also will benefit in several ways. In addition to enhanced access to U.S. markets, the accord will strengthen and help stabilize the region. In turn, U.S. direct investment is likely to rise, satisfying a strong demand for capital there. Plus, the agreement supports democracy and economic reform—

all factors that lead to higher standards of living.

In 2004, the United States exported $15.7 billion in goods to DR-CAFTA countries. This is more than all U.S. goods exported to Eastern Europe, plus Austria, Denmark and Finland. For many U.S. firms both small and large, expanding into DR-CAFTA markets is very advantageous.

www.ingramcontent.com/pod-product-compliance
Lightning Source LLC
Chambersburg PA
CBHW031519270326
41930CB00006B/435